Sunset

Light Ways with
Beef, Lamb
& Pork

By the Editors of Sunset Books and Sunset Magazine

Sunset Publishing Corporation ■ Menlo Park, California

Satisfying main-dish soups can be low in fat, too. Colorful Albóndigas Soup (recipe on page 20) features rice-studded meatballs made with ground lean beef round.

LEAN MEATS FOR HEALTHY MEALS

Is there a way for the health-conscious cook to include steak, lamb chops, roast pork and sautéed veal in a balanced, lowfat diet? Yes, indeed!

Today, the animals that supply these meats are bred to be leaner than in the past. The key to healthy cooking is to control the amount of fat, especially saturated fat, in the meat you serve. You can do this in three ways: by choosing lean cuts of meat to cook, by cooking these meats without adding high-fat ingredients, and by limiting the amount of the meat portion.

As you use this book, you'll become a more savvy shopper as you learn how to select the leanest meat cuts at the supermarket. A nutrition score-card on page 5 compares various cuts of meat, and lean cuts are listed boldly at the beginning of each chapter. You'll find that the recipes in this collection use little additional fat, and what fat is used is unsaturated, in the form of margarine, olive oil, or salad oil. And you'll discover the best methods of cooking the leaner cuts to decrease the amount of fat yet retain the moist, juicy texture and satisfying flavor of the meat. The book also suggests ways to decrease the amount of fat for other, higher-fat, cuts of meat. Individual servings adhere to a 3 oz. limit for meat, rounding out the meal with foods from lower-fat food groups.

Preparation and cooking times accompany each recipe. We also provide a nutritional analysis (see page 9) prepared by Hill Nutrition Associates, Inc., of Florida.

We extend our thanks to Barbara Szerlip for editing the manuscript. We also wish to thank Fillamento and Biordi Italian Imports for sharing props used in our photographs.

Research & Text
Cynthia Scheer

Coordinating Editor
Deborah Thomas Kramer

Design & Illustrations
Sandra Popovich

Photography
Nikolay Zurek

Photo Styling
Susan Massey-Weil

About the Recipes

All of the recipes in this book were tested and developed in the Sunset test kitchens.

Food and Entertaining Editor, Sunset Magazine
Jerry Anne Di Vecchio

Cover: Citrus-seasoned Steak & Brown Rice (recipe on page 33). Design by Susan Bryant. Photography by Nikolay Zurek. Photo styling by Susan Massey-Weil. Food styling by Cynthia Scheer.

Editor, Sunset Books: Elizabeth L. Hogan

Third printing September 1991

Contents

Special Features

Lean Meats

**Light ways to cook & serve
beef, lamb, pork & veal
with less fat, fewer calories**

Many a great cook has built a reputation on succulent, perfectly cooked and seasoned steak, lamb chops, roast pork, and sautéed veal. Is there a place for such cooking in a healthy, balanced, lowfat diet? Absolutely—for today the animals that supply these meats are all bred to be leaner than in the past. Nutritionally, meat has always been a superb source of complete protein.

Meat also supplies important B vitamins, as well as zinc and iron—minerals that meatless regimens may lack. In red meats, iron occurs in a form that's especially usable by the body, and meat even helps iron from other food sources to be utilized.

■ The nature of meat

That slice of roast or sizzling chop on your dinner plate is composed of muscles and fat held together by connective tissue. As we've become more health conscious, we've learned that the fat can cause trouble and that it's important to limit the amount of saturated fat and cholesterol in our diet.

Saturated fats, usually solid at room temperature, are typically found in foods of animal origin—meat and whole-milk dairy products are prime sources. Dietary cholesterol also is present in all animal-based foods—again, in meat and dairy products, and also in eggs.

But you can control the amount of fat in the meat you serve. First, choose lean meat to cook. At the beginning of each chapter in this book, we list the leanest cuts and indicate the part of the animal from which each comes.

Second, cook these meats without adding high-fat ingredients. Select one of several appropriate methods for a particular cut. Directions in each recipe describe the specific technique called for; you'll also find the cooking methods explained in general terms on pages 6, 8, and 9.

Third, limit the size of the meat portion. Nutritionally speaking, the ideal serving of cooked meat is 3 ounces (this translates to 4 ounces raw, boneless, fat-trimmed meat).

To compare the approximate number of calories and the amounts of fat and cholesterol in various meat

(Continued on page 6)

Nutritional Scorecard for Meats

Meat cut	Calories	Total Fat (grams)	Saturated Fat (grams)	Protein (grams)	Cholesterol (milligrams)
■ Beef					
Eye of round, roasted	143	4	1.5	25	59
Top round, broiled	153	4	1.4	27	71
Round tip, roasted	157	6	2.1	24	69
Sirloin steak, broiled	166	6	2.4	26	76
Flank steak, broiled	176	9	3.7	23	57
Bottom round, braised	178	7	2.4	27	82
Tenderloin, broiled	179	9	3.2	24	71
Liver, pan-fried	185	7	2.4	23	410
Porterhouse steak, broiled	185	9	3.7	24	68
Brisket, braised	189	8	2.7	27	81
Rib, roasted	195	11	4.2	23	68
Lean ground beef, broiled (15% fat)	204	12	4.8	22	71
Chuck blade, roasted	213	11	4.3	26	90
Regular ground beef, broiled (27% fat)	246	18	6.9	20	77
Short ribs, braised	251	15	6.6	26	79
■ Lamb					
Leg (shank portion), roasted	153	6	2.0	24	74
Foreshank, braised	159	5	1.8	26	88
Leg (sirloin portion), roasted	174	8	2.8	24	78
Shoulder blade chop, broiled	179	10	3.4	22	77
Loin chop, broiled	184	8	3.0	26	81
Rib, rack, roasted	197	11	4.1	22	75
Shoulder arm chop, braised	237	12	4.3	30	103
■ Pork					
Tenderloin, roasted	141	4	1.4	24	79
Leg, rump portion, roasted	187	9	3.2	24	80
Loin, center-cut, broiled	196	9	3.1	27	83
Loin, center rib chop, broiled	219	13	4.4	25	80
Loin, blade (country ribs), broiled	255	18	6.3	21	85
Shoulder, blade (butt), braised	316	24	8.8	22	95
Spareribs, braised (lean and fat)	338	26	10.0	25	103
■ Veal					
Rib, roasted	151	6	1.8	22	98
Leg cutlet, pan-fried	156	4	1.1	28	91
Shoulder blade steak, braised	168	6	1.5	28	134
Shoulder arm steak, braised	171	5	1.3	30	132
Sirloin chop, braised	174	6	1.6	29	96
Loin chop, braised	192	8	2.2	29	106

Figures for each cut are for a 3-ounce cooked portion with knife-separable fat removed.

cuts, take a look at the nutritional scorecard on page 5. It shows, in ascending order, a representative group of meat cuts by calorie count in each category.

■ Buying meat

How much meat should you buy to yield that model 3-ounce serving of cooked meat? It depends on the nature of the cut. Lean, boneless meat with little or no fat—such as ground meat, fillets, or boned, rolled roasts—will yield four such servings to a pound.

For meat with a medium amount of bone and some fat at the edges—loin and rib roasts, steaks, and chops—estimate 6 to 8 ounces per serving as purchased. With very bony cuts, such as veal or lamb shanks or breast, you'll need to buy 12 ounces to a pound to achieve a 3-ounce serving of cooked meat.

On most meat packages, the label now states more than just the weight and price. Under a new uniform meat labeling program, adopted by most retail food stores nationwide, even a beginning meat shopper can learn enough to help in making good choices.

A label like the one shown in the box below identifies the meat, states the part of the animal from which it was taken (an important clue to estimating the leanness of the meat), and gives the standard retail name for the cut. In addition, a retailer may show on the label or with a separate sticker some other familiar name for the cut—such as "London broil" for top round. Another sticker can also suggest good ways to cook a less familiar cut.

Date: when meat was packaged or last date it should be sold; if you're not sure, ask meatman

Universal Product Code, for electronic identification of the product

Kind of meat: beef, veal, pork, or lamb

The primal (wholesale) cut the piece came from

Standard retail name for cut taken from the primal part

■ What is the ideal fat intake?

All our recipes were calculated to contain 15 grams of fat or less, including the 3-ounce cooked serving of meat and all other required ingredients. That amount of fat accounts for a maximum of 135 calories (figure 9 calories for each gram of fat).

The American Heart Association and National Research Council recommend a daily fat intake of 30% or less of total calories, with less than 10% from saturated fat.

If a person consumes 2,000 calories a day, about 67 grams of fat supplies 30% of the day's calorie allotment; a 1,500-calorie diet allows about 50 grams of fat.

What little fat we've used in these recipes is unsaturated, in the form of margarine, olive oil, or salad oil. Remember that each teaspoon you use in cooking (beyond the amount specified in the recipe), or use to embellish other foods, adds another 5 grams of fat.

■ The best ways to cook lean meat

The two broadest categories for cooking meat are dry heat and moist heat. Dry-heat methods include roasting, broiling or grilling, and sautéing. Cooking with moist heat is also called braising, stewing, and simmering—in short, any technique by which meat is cooked in liquid.

In cooking today's lean meats, we've taken some liberties with the traditional definitions of these methods. Before we explain them, let's consider what happens when meat cooks.

As the internal temperature of meat increases, the fibers that comprise the meat shorten and bond, becoming more solid, and—at high temperatures—squeezing out liquid contained in the meat. That's why even the most naturally tender lean meat yields more willingly to the fork and exudes more juices when cooked only to the rare or medium-rare stage. It also explains why less-tender meat achieves greatest tenderness when it's cooked at a gentle temperature in a quantity of liquid.

Fat deposited within and surrounding meat, even when not visible, melts during cooking. This lubricates the meat fibers, making the meat seem more tender—and adding to the flavor. Recipes for today's lean meats, which lack much of this marbling and envelope of fat, must compensate for the absence of these fatty juices by other ingenious means. Of course, it can't be done by adding fat in other forms, such as bathing in an oily marinade or drenching in a creamy sauce—not if the overall goal of consuming less total fat is to be met.

Roasting. This is the technique by which meat is cooked, uncovered, by dry heat, usually in an oven. Cooking in a covered barbecue using indirect heat

(Continued on page 8)

Brandied Dijon Beef Stew (recipe on page 43)
demonstrates the delicious result of the lowfat technique
called "sweating"—braising bite-size pieces of less tender meat with
no flour, no frying, and an abundance of flavor.

(coals at either side of the grill, with meat above a drip pan in the center of the grill) also qualifies as roasting.

To roast lean meat, insert a meat thermometer in the thickest part (not touching bone). If using a glaze or sweet baste, line the roasting pan with foil or spray with vegetable oil cooking spray (or use a roasting pan with a nonstick surface). Place meat on a rack in the prepared pan.

The usual oven temperature recommended for achieving moist, juicy roasts is 325°. However, our mini-roasts (1- to 1¾-pound weight) cook so quickly that they need a higher oven temperature to brown attractively—425° for lamb or beef and 350° for pork. Pork tenderloin, which also can be roasted whole, is another cut that fares better at the relatively high temperature of 425°.

After the desired internal temperature is attained, lift the meat onto a carving board or platter. Cover the meat lightly with foil to keep it warm, and let stand for 5 to 15 minutes, depending on the size of the roast. This allows the juices to settle before the meat is sliced or carved, a step that makes the meat seem more succulent.

Broiling and grilling. To broil, select a shallow pan with a rack; grease the rack lightly, and place the meat on the rack. Position the pan below the heat source in your broiler, adjusting the pan or the oven rack until the top of the meat is the recommended distance below the heat. Remove the meat and preheat the broiler following the manufacturer's directions for your range. Broil, turning according to recipe directions. Test doneness by cutting in the center of the thickest part of the meat.

You can grill meat indoors or out. Some ranges have a built-in grill top, used in much the same way as a barbecue. You can also achieve grilled-looking meat with a heavy, cast-iron, ridged cooktop grill pan. Using such a pan is, in effect, pan-broiling. When you cook lean meats this way, it's a good idea to coat the cooking surface of the grill pan with a cooking spray to prevent sticking. Preheat the pan at the heat specified in the recipe until a few drops of water dance on the pan's surface.

Cooking meat on an outdoor barbecue is just like broiling in reverse; the meat cooks at a prescribed distance above the heat of the burning coals rather than below the heat source. Usually you can barbecue directly on the surface of the grill; grease it lightly to prevent lean meats from sticking.

Regulate the heat of the fire by the number of briquets you use and by how long you let them burn before cooking. For a *hot* fire, let the coals burn until they are just covered with gray ash (you can't hold your hand near the grill for more than 2 to 3 seconds); *medium* describes coals that glow through a layer of gray ash (you can't hold your hand near the grill for

Fat-lowering Strategies for Higher-fat Meats

When you're confronted with a cut of meat other than the lowfat cuts for which recipes are given, here are some ways you can prepare the meat in order to reduce unwanted fat.

■ Trim surface fat scrupulously.

■ Cook the meat in a way that renders the intramuscular fat. For example, you can pour off and discard drippings that remain after browning meats for stew or pot roast or ground meat dishes. Better yet, use our "sweating" method of moist-heat cooking (page 9); after the meat has cooked in its own juices for the first 30 minutes, lift it out with a slotted spoon, skim and discard the fat from the cooking liquid, then return the meat to the pan and continue cooking as directed.

■ Skim and discard fat from roasted meat drippings before adding liquid to the roasting pan to make gravy or sauce.

■ Make stews and soups ahead so that you can refrigerate them until thoroughly chilled. The fat that rises to the surface and hardens is then easier to lift off and discard, leaving a leaner dish to reheat.

■ Limit meat to a 3-ounce serving per person; it provides ample protein. Fill out the meal with foods from lower-fat food groups: complex carbohydrates, such as steamed rice, baked white or sweet potatoes, or your favorite pasta; green and yellow vegetables; leafy salads with lowfat dressings; fresh seasonal fruits; whole grain breads.

more than 4 to 5 seconds); *low* coals are covered with a thick layer of gray ash (you should be able to hold your hand near the grill for 6 to 7 seconds).

Adjust the cooking temperature by opening or closing any dampers on the barbecue.

Sautéing (panfrying). Cooks who sauté in the conventional way are likely to use more fat than fits into a 50- to 67-gram daily allowance. But there are ways to stay within the limits, especially when you cook very lean meats. A heavy frying pan with a good nonstick surface helps. Then, depending on the amount of meat to be cooked, either mist it with vegetable oil cooking spray or swirl in a very small amount (start with as little as

½ teaspoon) of oil or margarine as you preheat the pan at the recommended heat level. Turn the meat as soon as each side reaches the desired shade of brown; be careful not to overcook the thinner cuts of meat that are usually the best choices for sautéing.

When you are cooking more than two or three servings, it's best to sauté the meat in batches. Crowding the pan causes the cooking temperature to drop so much that the meat exudes juices and tends to seem hard and dry when cooked.

You can even produce lower-fat stir-fried dishes using this technique. Use tongs or a wide spatula to lift and turn the strips of meat.

Braising (stewing, simmering). These three moist-heat cooking methods are roughly similar; the only difference is in the amount of liquid involved—braising uses the least, simmering the most. Results range from a saucy stew, with just enough liquid to pool slightly around the meat and any added vegetables, to a brothy soup to eat with a spoon.

Lean cuts of meat that resist tenderizing by other methods will relax as they bubble ever so slightly over low heat in a well-seasoned liquid. The process takes time, but it usually needs very little attention after you've put all of the ingredients together. And dishes prepared in this style usually taste just as good, if not better, when cooked several hours or even a day ahead and then gently reheated.

Done in the traditional manner, this type of cooking needs a fair amount of fat to brown the meat. But we've discovered a slick way to do it with far less. It's called, rather inelegantly, "sweating." Instead of browning the meat first, a messy chore at best, you combine it with a small amount of water or other liquid, cover the pan, and "sweat" out the meat juices over medium-low heat.

Next you uncover the pan, increase the heat slightly, and let the meat juices cook away. The rendered drippings that remain become brown in the process, forming a savory coating for the meat. Then you add seasonings, more liquid, and vegetables that need long cooking. Vegetables that cook quickly are added toward the end, as is any needed thickening agent, such as flour or cornstarch.

As a variation, we've discovered a method of oven-braising (see Easy Oven Beef Stew, page 27, and Cider-baked Lamb Stew with Turnips, page 54). Brown flour-dusted cubes of the meat in a baking dish in a hot oven, then add liquid and vegetables to bake in the covered casserole.

■ Tools for light cooking

When you cook a cut of lean meat of any size and thickness, an accurate *meat thermometer* is essen-tial to tell you the internal temperature. That's very important, because just a few extra minutes in the oven or under the broiler can result in overcooking that dries out and toughens the meat.

Vegetable oil cooking spray prevents lean meat from sticking to the cooking pan or rack, whether you're cooking it in a frying pan, in a Dutch oven, or on the barbecue grill. For added flavor, use olive oil spray, now also available in this useful form. Some cooks like to spray one of these cooking oils on well-trimmed roasts to promote browning while adding only a whisper of fat.

A *roasting rack* elevates roasting meat above any fatty drippings so that the meat doesn't reabsorb them. If you can find a rack covered with nonstick coating, it will be easier to clean after each use.

Because our 3-ounce servings are less substantial than many hearty meat eaters may be accustomed to, a *sharp carving knife* or electric knife is a must. It enables you to cut neat, thin slices; visualize a 3-ounce serving of boneless meat as the size of a deck of playing cards.

Nonstick pans are a ready answer to the problem of how to cook lean meat in a scant amount of fat. A heavy pan is a good investment for the kitchen because it is less likely to warp, enabling meat to brown evenly. Frying pans with nonstick coatings are plentiful; it's worth seeking out a larger, deeper covered pan such as a Dutch oven with a nonstick coating, as well. Nonstick-coated roasting pans also have many advantages.

To preserve the expensive surface of your nonstick pans, use *nonmetal spatulas, tongs, and spoons* for lifting, turning, and stirring.

About Our Nutritional Data

For our recipes, we provide a nutritional analysis stating calorie count; grams of protein, carbohydrates, total fat, and saturated fat; and milligrams of cholesterol and sodium. Generally, the analysis applies to a single serving, based on the number of servings given for each recipe and the amount of each ingredient. If a range is given for the number of servings and/or the amount of an ingredient, the analysis is based on an average of the figures given.

The nutritional analysis does not include optional ingredients or those for which no specific amount is stated. If an ingredient is listed with a substitution, the information was calculated using the first choice.

One of the most luscious—and yet reassuringly lean—of all steaks takes center stage in Sautéed Fillet Steaks with Wild Rice & Baby Carrots (recipe on page 13). To complete the meal, add steamed pattypan or other summer squash and your favorite red wine.

Beef

Tenderloin
Top Loin
Sirloin
Flank Steak
Round Tip
Top Round
Eye of Round
Bottom Round
Center-cut Brisket
Lean Ground Beef

Today's beef comes from cattle bred for lean meat—meat that's as much as 10 percent leaner than 30 years ago and that has less marbling (the tiny streaks of fat that interlace the muscle). Fat content varies from place to place on the same animal, however, so it's important to choose your cuts wisely. (It's also important to cook lean cuts in ways that retain tenderness and flavor.) The illustration on page 12 shows where the lean cuts are located.

Lean Beef Cuts

Tenderloin. Meat from the loin is costly, but very tender and juicy. When conscientiously trimmed of outside fat, it can be included in a lowfat diet. Choose a cooking method that adds little or no fat: broiling, barbecuing, or sautéing in a nonstick pan with a vegetable oil cooking spray. Other names for this cut include filet mignon, fillet steak, medallion, and tenderloin tip.

Top Loin. Top loin steak is the larger portion of a sirloin or porterhouse, separated from the tenderloin by a center bone. Nearly as tender as tenderloin, top loin is considered by many people to have the better flavor. After trimming visible fat, cook it whole by broiling, barbecuing, or sautéing in a nonstick pan with a vegetable oil cooking spray. Sliced thinly, it can be stir-fried or threaded onto skewers. Cubed, it makes excellent kebabs. This cut is sometimes labeled New York, Delmonico, club, or strip steak.

Sirloin. The largest of the loin steaks, sirloin is comprised of several tender, juicy, and flavorful muscles which are usually sold separately as top sirloin, fillet, and culotte steak. All can be cooked by dry-heat methods: broiling, barbecuing, sautéing in a nonstick pan with vegetable oil cooking spray, or stir-frying.

Flank Steak. Robustly flavored flank steak comes from the area below the loin. It has a coarser, more fibrous texture than the loin and is considerably less tender. When cooked by dry-heat methods (broiling, barbecuing, sautéing, stir-frying), it should be either marinated or cooked to the rare or medium-rare stage only. If you prefer your beef well-done, cook the meat by a moist-heat method.

Round Tip. The round is lean and mild in flavor. The entire round can be seen clearly in cross section, muscle by muscle, in a full-cut round steak; it consists of round tip (often sold as sirloin tip), top round, eye of round, and bottom round. Round tip is the most tender of the four. It can be oven-roasted whole if cooked only to the rare or medium-rare stage and is also a good candidate for braising, stewing, or pot roasting.

Top Round. This second-most-tender portion of the round is often served as London broil, sliced thinly across the grain at a slant. Cut into cubes or strips and marinated, top round can also be barbecued, and it's a good choice for simmering or stewing.

Eye of Round. This very lean, compact, and finely grained portion of the round needs help to be fork-tender. When sautéing, first pound the meat well to break down the connective tissue. Moist-heat methods, such as braising, also contribute to tenderness. Eye of round is sold either as a roast or cut into portion-size steaks.

Bottom Round. Though similar to eye of round in tenderness, bottom round is more flavorful and has a coarser grain. It's best cooked by moist heat—braised or stewed in a flavorful liquid.

Center-cut Brisket. Brisket comes from the forequarter between the chuck and the shank; preserved in brine, it becomes corned beef. Similar in texture to flank steak, it is considerably less tender. Moist-heat cooking methods are best, although brisket can also be treated with meat tenderizer and barbecued to the rare or medium-rare stage.

Lean Ground Beef. To be sure ground beef is truly lean (less than 15% fat), insist on well-trimmed meat from the round. You can grind your own using the method described for lamb on page 60.

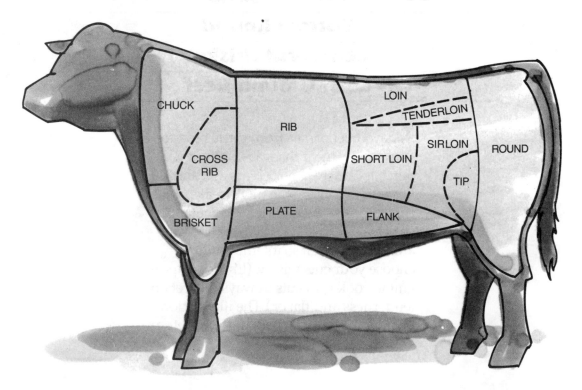

Grilled Herbed Tenderloin with Arugula

Preparation time: About 10 minutes

Cooking time: About 5 minutes

Quickly cooked fillets nestle atop pungent arugula in a tart-sweet balsamic vinegar sauce.

- 1 teaspoon dry rosemary
- 1 tablespoon slivered fresh sage leaves or 1 teaspoon dry sage leaves
- 4 beef tenderloin steaks (about 1 lb. *total*), trimmed of fat

    Coarsely ground pepper

- 1 bunch arugula or watercress (10 to 12 oz.), washed, crisped, and stemmed

    Olive oil cooking spray

    Salt

- 1½ tablespoons balsamic vinegar or red wine vinegar
- 1½ tablespoons olive oil

    Lemon wedges

Combine rosemary and sage. Coat steaks on both sides with herb mixture; season to taste with pepper, pressing pepper into the meat. Arrange arugula on 4 dinner plates and set aside.

Coat a ridged rangetop grill pan with cooking spray. Place pan over medium-high heat until hot. Add steaks and cook, turning once, until well browned (4 to 6 minutes *total* for rare to medium-rare). Lift steaks from pan and season to taste with salt; then place atop arugula.

Remove pan from heat. Drizzle vinegar over drippings, stirring to loosen any browned bits; then pour into a small bowl. Stir in oil. Drizzle vinegar mixture over arugula and meat. Garnish with lemon wedges. Makes 4 servings.

■ *Per serving: 238 calories, 25 g protein, 1 g carbohydrates, 14 g total fat (4 g saturated fat), 70 mg cholesterol, 91 mg sodium*

■ *Pictured on page 10*

Sautéed Fillet Steaks with Wild Rice & Baby Carrots

Preparation time: About 15 minutes

Cooking time: About 50 minutes

Begin cooking the herbed rice first. When it's nearly done, sauté the mustard-laced fillets, then add vermouth and capers to drippings for an elegant sauce.

- 1½ tablespoons margarine
- ½ cup wild rice, rinsed and drained
- 1 teaspoon herbes de Provence or Italian herb seasoning
- 1½ cups regular-strength chicken broth
- 1 bunch baby carrots (about 8 oz. with tops)
- ¼ teaspoon ground white pepper
- 1 teaspoon Dijon mustard
- 4 beef tenderloin steaks (about 1 lb. *total*), trimmed of fat
- 2 tablespoons lemon juice

    Salt

- ⅓ cup dry vermouth
- 2 teaspoons capers

    Italian parsley sprigs

    Lemon wedges

In a 10-inch frying pan, melt ½ tablespoon of the margarine over medium-high heat; stir in rice and herbes de Provence. Cook, stirring, for about 1 minute. Add chicken broth; reduce heat, cover, and simmer for 35 minutes. Arrange carrots over rice and sprinkle with pepper. Cover and continue cooking until rice and carrots are tender to bite (10 to 15 minutes).

When rice is almost done, melt remaining 1 tablespoon margarine in a wide nonstick frying pan over medium-high heat; stir in mustard. Add steaks and cook, turning once, until well browned (4 to 6 minutes *total* for rare to medium-rare). Lift from pan and keep warm.

Gently stir lemon juice into rice mixture; spoon onto a warm platter. Season steaks to taste with salt and arrange on platter with rice and carrots. Add vermouth and capers to meat drippings. Bring to a boil, stirring, and continue boiling for 2 minutes. Spoon vermouth mixture over steaks, rice, and carrots. Garnish with parsley and lemon wedges. Makes 4 servings.

■ *Per serving: 360 calories, 28 g protein, 24 g carbohydrates, 14 g total fat (4 g saturated fat), 70 mg cholesterol, 580 mg sodium*

Marsala & Mushroom Steaks

Preparation time: About 5 minutes

Cooking time: About 15 minutes

A quick yet elegant entrée for two, this recipe contains surprisingly little fat. A generous topping of sautéed mushrooms and marsala-laced meat juices makes this an easy dish for a special occasion.

> 2 teaspoons margarine
> ½ pound mushrooms, sliced
> Vegetable oil cooking spray
> 2 beef tenderloin steaks (about 8 oz. *total*), trimmed of fat
> Salt and pepper
> 3 tablespoons Marsala
> Watercress sprigs, washed and crisped

In a wide nonstick frying pan, melt margarine over medium-high heat. Add mushrooms and cook, stirring often, until liquid has evaporated and mushrooms are browned (6 to 8 minutes). Lift mushrooms from pan and keep warm. Coat pan with cooking spray. Add steaks and cook, turning once, until well browned (4 to 6 minutes *total* for rare to medium-rare). Place steaks on a warm platter and season to taste with salt and pepper; then top with mushrooms.

Add Marsala to drippings in pan and bring to a boil, stirring to loosen any browned bits. Spoon Marsala mixture over steaks and mushrooms. Garnish with watercress. Makes 2 servings.

■ *Per serving: 282 calories, 26 g protein, 8 g carbohydrates, 14 g total fat (4 g saturated fat), 70 mg cholesterol, 112 mg sodium*

■ *Pictured on facing page*

Barbecued Sirloin with Scorched Corn & Chile Salsa

Preparation time: About 25 minutes

Marinating time: At least 2 hours

Grilling time: 8 to 10 minutes

A red wine marinade flavored with cumin and cinnamon adds a Southwestern accent to this steak. It cooks on the barbecue with fresh corn, which is added to the piquant tomato salsa. Spoon salsa over the sliced steak, and use it as a topping for baked potatoes to accompany the meat.

> Cumin-Cinnamon Marinade (recipe follows)
> 1 pound boneless sirloin steak (about ¾ inch thick), trimmed of fat
> 1 small tomato, seeded and finely chopped
> 1 medium-size fresh Anaheim (California) green chile, seeded and finely chopped
> 2 cloves garlic, minced or pressed
> 2 tablespoons lime juice
> 1 tablespoon ground New Mexico or California chiles
> 2 medium-size ears corn
> Salt
> Lime slices

Prepare Cumin-Cinnamon Marinade; add steak. Cover and refrigerate for at least 2 hours or until next day. Shortly before cooking steak, combine tomato, chopped chile, garlic, lime juice, and ground chiles; set aside.

Remove and discard husks and silk from corn. Lift steak from bowl, reserving marinade. Place steak and corn on a lightly greased grill 4 to 6 inches above a solid bed of medium-hot coals. Cook, drizzling steak several times with marinade and turning once, and turning corn as needed, until both are browned (8 to 10 minutes *total* for rare to medium-rare steak, about 8 minutes *total* for corn).

Place steak on a carving board and keep warm. Cut corn from cobs and stir into tomato mixture; season to taste with salt. Slice or quarter steak and garnish with lime slices; serve with salsa. Makes 4 servings.

Cumin-Cinnamon Marinade. In a shallow glass bowl, combine ½ cup **dry red wine;** 1 tablespoon **olive oil;** 2 tablespoons finely chopped **onion;** 2 cloves **garlic,** minced or pressed; ¼ teaspoon **salt;** ½ teaspoon *each* **ground cumin** and **ground cinnamon;** and 1½ teaspoons **cumin seeds.**

■ *Per serving: 222 calories, 26 g protein, 13 g carbohydrates, 8 g total fat (2 g saturated fat), 69 mg cholesterol, 148 mg sodium*

Hot from the grill, spicy Barbecued Sirloin with
Scorched Corn & Chile Salsa (recipe on facing page) makes a handsome
and substantial entrée reminiscent of the Southwest. Serve additional
salsa to spoon over baked potatoes.

Lean Sirloin Stroganoff

Preparation time: About 15 minutes

Cooking time: About 10 minutes

Substitute thickened yogurt for the traditional sour cream to keep this elegant dish within the boundaries of lowfat cooking.

- 1 **pound boneless sirloin steak, trimmed of fat**
- 2 **to 3 teaspoons salad oil**
- ⅓ **cup thinly sliced shallots or sweet red onion**
- ½ **pound mushrooms, thinly sliced**
- 1 **package (9 oz.) fresh fettuccine or 8 ounces dry fettuccine**
- 2 **teaspoons Worcestershire**
- ¼ **teaspoon sweet Hungarian paprika**
- ⅛ **teaspoon white pepper**
- ¼ **cup dry vermouth**
- ¾ **cup plain lowfat yogurt blended with 1 tablespoon cornstarch**
- ¼ **teaspoon sugar**
  Salt
  Chopped parsley

Slice steak into bite-size strips about ⅛ inch thick. Heat 1 teaspoon of the oil in a wide nonstick frying pan over medium-high heat. Add half the steak. Cook, stirring, just until strips are browned on all sides; remove from pan. Repeat with 1 more teaspoon of the oil and remaining steak.

Add shallots and mushrooms to pan with remaining teaspoon oil, if needed. Cook, stirring, until most of the liquid has evaporated and mushrooms are browned. Meanwhile, in a 5- to 6-quart pan, cook fettuccine in 3 quarts boiling water just until tender (3 to 4 minutes for fresh pasta, 8 to 10 minutes for dry); or cook according to package directions.

To mushroom mixture add Worcestershire, paprika, pepper, and vermouth. Blend in yogurt mixture and sugar. Cook, stirring, until sauce is bubbling and has thickened. Return meat to pan, stirring to coat, and cook just until heated through (about 1 minute). Season to taste with salt. Drain pasta and place on a platter. Top with meat mixture and garnish with parsley. Makes 4 servings.

■ *Per serving: 443 calories, 36 g protein, 47 g carbohydrates, 10 g total fat (3 g saturated fat), 147 mg cholesterol, 146 mg sodium*

Grilled Top Sirloin with Wine–Shallot Sauce

Preparation time: About 10 minutes

Grilling time: About 20 minutes

Tantalizing aromas greet your dinner guests as sweet red onion halves grill around a thick, boneless steak. A savory wine sauce, brimming with chopped shallots, bubbles alongside; at serving time, it's spooned over both steak and onions.

- 1 **to 1½ pounds boneless top sirloin steak (1½ to 2 inches thick), trimmed of fat**
- 2 **or 3 small red onions (about 5 oz. *each*), unpeeled, cut in half lengthwise**
- 1 **tablespoon margarine**
- ½ **cup chopped shallots**
- ¾ **cup dry red wine**
- 1 **tablespoon Dijon mustard**
- 1 **teaspoon Worcestershire**
- ½ **teaspoon *each* coarsely ground pepper and dry tarragon leaves**
  Salt

Place steak on a lightly greased grill 4 to 6 inches above a solid bed of medium coals. Place onions, cut sides down, on grill. Cook, turning both steak and onions after about 10 minutes, until a thermometer inserted in thickest part of steak registers 135° to 140° for rare and onions are soft when pressed (18 to 20 minutes *total*).

Meanwhile, melt margarine in a small, metal-handled frying pan on grill; add shallots and cook, stirring occasionally, until tinged with brown (6 to 8 minutes). Add wine, mustard, Worcestershire, pepper, and tarragon. Cook, stirring often, until sauce is reduced to about ½ cup (about 10 minutes); then move to a cooler part of grill.

Transfer steak and onions to a platter. Slice steak thinly across grain at a slant. If desired, stir accumulated meat juices into sauce. Season sauce to taste with salt and spoon over steak and onions. Makes 4 to 6 servings.

■ *Per serving: 231 calories, 27 g protein, 9 g carbohydrates, 9 g total fat (3 g saturated fat), 76 mg cholesterol, 189 mg sodium*

Barbecued Steak au Poivre

Preparation time: About 10 minutes

Standing time: At least 30 minutes

Grilling time: 8 to 10 minutes

Sirloin steak sprinkled with crushed black peppercorns shares the barbecue grill with thick tomato slices. Just before serving, pour flaming brandy over both the steak and tomatoes.

- 1 **pound boneless top sirloin steak (¾ to 1 inch thick), trimmed of fat**
- 1½ **teaspoons whole black peppercorns, coarsely crushed**
- 2 **large tomatoes (about 1 lb. *total*)**
  Olive oil cooking spray
- 2 **tablespoons slivered fresh basil leaves or ½ teaspoon dry basil leaves**
- 2 **cloves garlic, minced or pressed**
  Salt
- ¼ **cup brandy**
  Basil sprigs

Cut steak into 4 portions. Press crushed pepper into both sides of each piece. Cover and refrigerate for 30 minutes to 1 hour.

Meanwhile, cut each tomato into 4 equal slices and arrange in a single layer in a shallow pan. Spray tomatoes lightly with cooking spray and sprinkle with basil leaves and garlic. Set aside.

Place steaks on a lightly greased grill 4 to 6 inches above a solid bed of medium-hot coals. Cook, turning once, until browned (8 to 10 minutes *total* for rare to medium-rare). When steaks are turned, place tomatoes, seasoned sides down, around them on grill. Transfer cooked steaks to a platter and keep warm. Turn tomato slices to warm unseasoned sides; then arrange around steaks. Season to taste with salt.

In a small, long-handled metal pan at edge of grill, heat brandy just until barely warm to touch (about 30 seconds). Ignite; then pour, flaming, over steak and tomatoes. Garnish with basil sprigs. Makes 4 servings.

■ *Per serving: 215 calories, 27 g protein, 6 g carbohydrates, 7 g total fat (2 g saturated fat), 76 mg cholesterol, 66 mg sodium*

Pakistani Beef Kebabs

Preparation time: About 15 minutes

Marinating time: At least 8 hours

Grilling time: 8 to 10 minutes

Marinate steak cubes in a spicy yogurt mixture, then thread meat onto long skewers for grilling. Cubes of lean boneless lamb leg or shoulder can also be used to make kebabs.

- 1 **cup plain lowfat yogurt**
- 1 **small onion, finely chopped**
- 1 **clove garlic, minced or pressed**
- 1 **teaspoon grated fresh ginger or ¼ teaspoon ground ginger**
- 1 **small dried hot red chile, crushed**
- ½ **teaspoon cumin seeds, coarsely crushed**
- ¼ **teaspoon *each* ground nutmeg, ground cardamom, and salt**
- ⅛ **teaspoon *each* ground cinnamon, ground cloves, and coarsely ground pepper**
- 1½ **pounds boneless top sirloin steak, trimmed of fat**

In a 2-quart bowl, combine yogurt, onion, garlic, ginger, chile, cumin, nutmeg, cardamom, salt, cinnamon, cloves, and pepper. Cut steak into 1-inch

cubes; stir into yogurt mixture. Cover and refrigerate, stirring once or twice, for at least 8 hours or until next day.

Lift meat from marinade and thread onto 6 skewers (*each* about 9 inches long). Place on a lightly greased grill 4 to 6 inches above a solid bed of medium-hot coals. Cook, turning skewers as needed, until meat is browned on all sides (8 to 10 minutes *total* for rare to medium-rare). Makes 6 servings.

■ *Per serving: 182 calories, 27 g protein, 2 g carbohydrates, 6 g total fat (3 g saturated fat), 77 mg cholesterol, 116 mg sodium*

*Marinate strips of top sirloin in a flavorful tart-sweet soy and honey
sauce, then thread them onto thin skewers to grill for Marinated Beef on
a Stick (recipe on facing page). Zucchini and small red onion halves cook
alongside the meat; brown rice steamed in beef broth completes the menu.*

Marinated Beef on a Stick

Preparation time: About 15 minutes

Marinating time: At least 1 hour

Grilling time: 4 to 5 minutes

Laced with garlic and ginger, the sweet-sour marinade flavors the thin slices of sirloin. Use thin skewers so beef strips will lie flat during grilling. Because the meat cooks quickly over hot coals, baste skewered beef frequently during cooking.

1½	**pounds boneless top sirloin steak, trimmed of fat**
½	**cup soy sauce**
1	**tablespoon salad oil**
2	**tablespoons *each* honey and red wine vinegar**
1	**clove garlic, minced or pressed**
¼	**teaspoon pepper**
½	**teaspoon ground ginger**

Cut steak across grain into ¼-inch-thick slices, each about 4 inches long (for easier slicing, partially freeze steak for 30 to 45 minutes first). In a bowl, combine steak, soy sauce, oil, honey, vinegar, garlic, pepper, and ginger; mix well. Cover and refrigerate for 1 to 2 hours.

Lift meat from bowl, reserving marinade. Weave strips onto thin skewers so meat lies flat, then place on a lightly greased grill 4 to 6 inches above a solid bed of hot coals. Cook, brushing often with marinade and turning each skewer once, until meat is browned (4 to 5 minutes *total* for medium-rare). Makes 6 servings.

■ *Per serving: 175 calories, 26 g protein, 1 g carbohydrates, 7 g total fat (2 g saturated fat), 76 mg cholesterol, 268 mg sodium*

Steak Mexicana

Preparation time: About 15 minutes

Cooking time: About 20 minutes

To give barbecued steaks a south-of-the-border flavor, top with a generous serving of this lively tomato and green chile sauce.

2	**teaspoons salad oil**
1	**small onion, finely chopped**
1	**canned California green chile, seeded and chopped**
¼	**teaspoon *each* salt and ground cumin**
1½	**cups peeled chopped tomatoes**
1	**pound boneless top sirloin steak (about ¾ inch thick), trimmed of fat**
¼	**cup shredded jack cheese**
	Lime wedges
	Cilantro (coriander) sprigs

Heat oil in a wide nonstick frying pan over medium heat. Add onion, chile, salt, and cumin. Cook, stirring often, until onion is soft and beginning to brown (3 to 5 minutes). Stir in tomatoes; increase heat to medium-high and cook, stirring often, until most of the liquid has evaporated (6 to 8 minutes). Keep sauce warm.

Cut steak into 4 portions. Place on a rack in a broiler pan. Broil about 4 inches below heat, turning once, until browned (4 to 6 minutes *total*). Spoon tomato sauce over steaks and top with cheese; broil until cheese is melted (1 to 2 minutes). Garnish with lime wedges and cilantro. Makes 4 servings.

■ *Per serving: 234 calories, 28 g protein, 5 g carbohydrates, 11 g total fat (3 g saturated fat), 82 mg cholesterol, 346 mg sodium*

Feature

Lean Beef Soups

Rib-sticking soups are favorite family fare, especially in cold weather. To ensure that what sticks to your ribs isn't fat, prepare these soups using the same cuts of beef you would choose for meatier dishes—well-trimmed round or the leanest ground beef. All of these full-meal soups can be made ahead and chilled. If any fat rises to the top and hardens during refrigeration, it can be skimmed off before reheating.

Goulash Soup

    1   pound boneless beef round tip, trimmed
        of fat
    2   medium-size onions, finely chopped
    1   clove garlic, minced or pressed
    1   teaspoon salad oil
    1   tablespoon sweet Hungarian paprika
    ½   teaspoon dry marjoram leaves
    5   cups water
    2   tablespoons all-purpose flour
    3   beef bouillon cubes
    2   small thin-skinned potatoes (about 12
        oz. *total*), cut into ½-inch cubes
    1   medium-size red bell pepper, seeded
        and finely chopped
        Salt and white pepper
    ¼   cup chopped parsley

Cut beef into ½-inch cubes. In a 3½- to 4-quart pan, combine beef, onions, garlic, oil, paprika, marjoram, and ½ cup of the water. Cover and simmer over medium-low heat for 30 minutes. Uncover and

increase heat to medium; cook, stirring often, until liquid has evaporated and onions are browned (20 to 25 minutes).

Stir in flour until smoothly blended. Add 1 cup more of the water and bouillon cubes, stirring to dissolve bouillon and loosen any browned bits in pan. Gradually blend in remaining 3½ cups water and bring to a boil. Add potatoes and bell pepper. Reduce heat, cover, and simmer, stirring occasionally, until meat is very tender (1 to 1½ hours). Skim and discard surface fat, if necessary. Season to taste with salt and pepper. Stir in parsley. Makes 4 servings.

■ *Per serving: 264 calories, 27 g protein, 24 g carbohydrates, 6 g total fat (2 g saturated fat), 68 mg cholesterol, 664 mg sodium*

■ *Pictured on page 2*

Albóndigas Soup

        Meatballs with Rice (recipe follows)
    1   tablespoon salad oil
    1   large onion, slivered
    1½ teaspoons ground cumin
    1   teaspoon dry oregano leaves
    2   cloves garlic, minced or pressed
    1   can (14½ oz.) pear-shaped tomatoes
    2   cans (14½ oz. *each*) regular-strength
        beef broth
    1   large can (46 oz.) low-sodium
        tomato juice
    ¼   cup coarsely chopped cilantro
        (coriander)
        Salt
    1   large lime, cut into 6 wedges

Prepare Meatballs with Rice.

While meatballs are baking, heat oil in a 5- to 6-quart pan over medium heat. Add onion, cumin, and oregano. Cook, stirring often, until onion is golden (6 to 8 minutes); then stir in garlic. Add tomatoes (break up with a spoon) and their liquid, beef broth, and tomato juice; cover, increase heat to high, and bring to a boil. Reduce heat, cover, and simmer for 15 minutes.

Loosen meatballs from baking pan with a wide spatula and transfer to soup. Cover and simmer until meatballs are heated through (about 10 minutes). Skim and discard surface fat, if necessary. Just before serving, stir in cilantro and season to taste with salt. Offer with lime. Makes 6 servings.

Meatballs with Rice. In a large bowl, lightly mix 1½ pounds **ground lean beef round**, ½ cup **cooked white or brown rice**, ¼ cup *each* **all-purpose flour and water**, and 1 teaspoon *each* **chili powder** and **ground cumin**. Shape mixture into 1-inch balls and place slightly apart in a nonstick shallow baking pan. Bake, uncovered, in a 450° oven until well browned (about 15 minutes).

■ *Per serving: 292 calories, 31 g protein, 27 g carbohydrates, 7 g total fat (2 g saturated fat), 65 mg cholesterol, 701 mg sodium*

Mexican Beef & Pork Birria

1	pound boneless beef top round, trimmed of fat
½	pound lean boneless pork, trimmed of fat
1	medium-size onion, thinly sliced
1	medium-size carrot, coarsely shredded
2	cloves garlic, minced or pressed
3	tablespoons chili powder
1	teaspoon *each* ground cumin and salad oil
4	cups water
2	cans (14½ oz. *each*) regular-strength beef broth
	Salt
	About ½ cup sliced green onions (including tops)
1	large lime, cut into 6 wedges

Cut beef and pork into 1-inch cubes. In a 3½- to 4-quart pan, combine meat with onion, carrot, garlic, chili powder, cumin, oil, and ½ cup of the water. Cover and simmer over medium-low heat for 30 minutes.

Uncover; increase heat to medium and cook, stirring often, until liquid has evaporated (20 to 25 minutes). Add 1 cup more of the water, stirring to loosen any browned bits in pan. Blend in remaining 2½ cups water and beef broth. Bring to a boil; then cover, reduce heat, and simmer until meat is very tender (about 1½ hours). Skim and discard surface

fat, if necessary. Season to taste with salt. Garnish with green onions and lime. Makes 6 servings.

■ *Per serving: 207 calories, 28 g protein, 7 g carbohydrates, 36 g total fat (2 g saturated fat), 67 mg cholesterol, 608 mg sodium*

Ground Beef & Vegetable Soup

	Olive oil cooking spray
1	pound ground lean beef round
1	medium-size onion, chopped
1	green bell pepper, seeded and chopped
1	tablespoon chili powder
2	cloves garlic, minced or pressed
1	large can (28 oz.) tomatoes
2	medium-size carrots (about 6 oz. *total*), thinly sliced
2	medium-size thin-skinned potatoes (about 12 oz. *total*), cut into ½-inch cubes
3	beef bouillon cubes
5	cups water
1	bay leaf
	About ½ teaspoon salt
¼	teaspoon pepper
1	package (10 oz.) frozen baby lima beans
½	small head cabbage, coarsely shredded (about 4 cups)
	Salt
½	to ¾ cup grated Parmesan cheese

Spray bottom of a deep 5- to 6-quart pan with cooking spray. Crumble in beef and cook over medium-high heat, stirring, until pink color is gone. Add onion, bell pepper, and chili powder; continue to cook, stirring, until onion is lightly browned (8 to 10 minutes). Mix in garlic. Add tomatoes (break up with a spoon) and their liquid, carrots, potatoes, and bouillon; stir until bouillon cubes have dissolved. Stir in water, bay leaf, salt, and pepper. Bring to a boil; then reduce heat, cover, and simmer for 1 hour. (At this point, you may let cool, cover, and refrigerate until next day.)

Stir in lima beans and cabbage. Increase heat to medium and cook, uncovered, just until cabbage is tender but still bright green (10 to 15 minutes). Skim and discard surface fat, if necessary. Season to taste with salt. Offer cheese to sprinkle over individual portions. Makes 6 to 8 servings.

■ *Per serving: 266 calories, 24 g protein, 31 g carbohydrates, 5 g total fat (2 g saturated fat), 43 mg cholesterol, 894 mg sodium*

Braised Top Sirloin Picante

Preparation time: About 15 minutes

Cooking time: About 1¾ hours

Cook top sirloin with wine, onion, chiles, pimentos, and garlic for a robust stew with a Mexican accent.

- 1½ **pounds boneless top sirloin steak, trimmed of fat**
- 1 **large onion, chopped**
- 1 **large clove garlic, minced or pressed**
- 1 **tablespoon salad oil**
- ½ **cup water**
- ¼ **teaspoon *each* pepper, dry oregano leaves, and ground cumin**
- 1½ **tablespoons chili powder**
- 1 **tablespoon catsup**
- ⅓ **cup dry red wine**
- 1 **can (4 oz.) diced green chiles**
- 1 **jar (2 oz.) sliced pimentos**
- 1 **can (14½ oz.) regular-strength beef broth**
  Chopped cilantro (coriander) or parsley
- 3 **cups hot cooked rice**

Cut steak into 1-inch cubes. In a heavy 3½- to 4-quart pan, combine steak, onion, garlic, oil, and water. Cover and cook over medium heat for 30 minutes. Uncover and continue cooking, stirring occasionally, until most of the liquid has evaporated and juices and onion are browned (25 to 30 minutes).

Stir in pepper, oregano, cumin, chili powder, catsup, wine, chiles, pimentos, and beef broth. Reduce heat, cover, and simmer until meat is very tender when pierced (about 45 minutes). Lift out meat with a slotted spoon, cover, and set aside. Increase heat to high and boil cooking liquid, stirring often, until reduced to about 2½ cups (3 to 5 minutes). Return meat to sauce, stirring just until heated through (1 to 2 minutes). Garnish with cilantro and serve with rice. Makes 6 servings.

■ *Per serving: 334 calories, 28 g protein, 35 g carbohydrates, 8 g total fat (2 g saturated fat), 69 mg cholesterol, 486 mg sodium*

■ *Pictured on facing page*

Lemon-broiled Flank Steak with Onions

Preparation time: About 10 minutes

Marinating time: At least 2 hours

Cooking time: 8 to 10 minutes

Generously flavored with lemon and herbs, this tangy marinade does double duty: It tenderizes the meat and is used in the onion topping

- 1 **to 1¼ pounds flank steak, trimmed of fat**
- 1 **large onion, thinly sliced**
- ⅓ **cup lemon juice**
- 1 **teaspoon Italian herb seasoning or ¼ teaspoon *each* dry basil, oregano, thyme, and marjoram leaves**
- 1 **teaspoon grated lemon peel**
- 1 **large clove garlic, minced or pressed**
- ¼ **teaspoon coarsely ground pepper**
- 2 **teaspoons sugar**
- 2 **tablespoons soy sauce**
- 1 **tablespoon olive oil**
  Lemon wedges (optional)
  Chopped parsley (optional)

Score steak on both sides about ⅛ inch deep in a 1-inch diamond pattern. In a shallow baking dish, spread half the onion; top with steak and add remaining onion. In a small bowl, stir together lemon juice, herb seasoning, lemon peel, garlic, pepper, sugar, and soy sauce. Pour over steak and onion. Cover and refrigerate for at least 2 hours or up to 8 hours.

Lift steak from dish, reserving marinade and onion. Place steak on a lightly greased rack in a broiler pan. Broil 3 to 4 inches below heat, turning once until browned; cut to test (8 to 10 minutes *total* for rare to medium).

Meanwhile, heat oil in a medium-size frying pan over medium-high heat. Add marinade and onion and bring to a boil. Cook, stirring often, until onion is soft and lightly browned and most of the liquid has evaporated (6 to 8 minutes). Slice steak thinly across grain at a slant. Spoon onions over top. Garnish with lemon wedges and parsley, if desired. Makes about 4 servings.

■ *Per serving: 211 calories, 22 g protein, 6 g carbohydrates, 11 g total fat (4 g saturated fat), 52 mg cholesterol, 483 mg sodium*

*The intense citrus flavor of marinated Lemon-broiled Flank Steak
with Onions (recipe on facing page) is a lively foil for spicy Curried New
Potatoes with Green Onions (recipe on page 29).*

West Indian Flank Steak Burritos

Preparation time: About 10 minutes

Marinating time: At least 30 minutes

Grilling time: About 15 minutes

A distinctive, bottled West Indian sauce of tamarinds, mangoes, and fiery peppers flavors this flank steak. Slice the barbecued meat thinly and spoon it into warm tortillas. Add onion and chopped tomato and roll up to eat.

- 1½ **pounds flank steak, trimmed of fat**
- 2 **to 3 tablespoons Jamaican hot pepper sauce with tamarind; or 2½ tablespoons bottled steak sauce mixed with liquid hot pepper seasoning to taste**
- 12 **flour tortillas (about 8-inch diameter)**
- 3 **small onions, unpeeled, cut in half lengthwise**
- 1 **large tomato (about 8 oz.), chopped**
   Salt
   Lime wedges

Place steak in a baking dish and brush both sides with sauce. Cover and refrigerate for at least 30 minutes or up to 2 hours. Wrap tortillas in foil and set aside. Place onions, cut sides down, on a lightly greased grill 4 to 6 inches above a solid bed of hot coals. Cook for about 7 minutes; then turn. Add steak to grill; place tortillas at side of grill away from highest heat. Continue cooking onions until soft and browned (5 to 9 more minutes). Cook steak, turning once, until browned (6 to 8 minutes *total* for rare). Turn tortilla packet several times until warm (5 to 10 minutes).

Cut onions into wedges. Slice steak thinly across grain at a slant. Place 2 or 3 steak slices on each tortilla, along with some of the onion and tomato. Season to taste with salt and lime. Roll up to eat. Makes 6 servings (2 burritos *each*).

■ *Per serving: 335 calories, 28 g protein, 28 g carbohydrates, 13 g total fat (4 g saturated fat), 57 mg cholesterol, 480 mg sodium*

Flank Steak with Asparagus & Mushrooms

Preparation time: About 20 minutes

Cooking time: About 15 minutes

This quick-cooking dish can be eaten with chopsticks, though its flavor is more French than Asian. Steam the asparagus first; then add it to the flank steak stir-fry.

- 1¼ **pounds asparagus**
- 1 **to 1¼ pounds flank steak, trimmed of fat**
- 1 **tablespoon cornstarch blended with ½ cup water**
- ⅓ **cup dry red wine**
- ½ **teaspoon *each* salt and dry tarragon leaves**
- 3 **teaspoons olive oil**
- ½ **pound mushrooms, thinly sliced**
- 1 **small onion, thinly sliced**
- 1 **large clove garlic, minced or pressed**
- ¼ **cup regular-strength beef broth**
- 2 **to 3 cups hot cooked brown rice**

Snap off and discard asparagus ends; cut stalks diagonally into ½-inch slices, leaving tips whole. Cut steak in half lengthwise; then slice each half diagonally into ¼-inch-thick strips and set aside. In a small bowl, stir together cornstarch mixture, wine, salt, and tarragon and set aside.

Place asparagus on a rack over ½ inch boiling water. Cover and steam over high heat until bright green and barely tender-crisp (2 to 3 minutes). Remove asparagus and set aside.

Heat 2 teaspoons of the oil in a wide nonstick frying pan over high heat. Add steak, about a fourth at a time. Cook, turning and stirring, just until strips are browned on all sides; lift out strips as they brown and add to asparagus. Repeat with remaining steak.

Place mushrooms and onion in pan with remaining 1 teaspoon oil. Cook, stirring, until most of the liquid has evaporated and mushrooms are browned (about 3 minutes). Add garlic, wine mixture, and beef broth; cook, stirring constantly, until sauce is bubbling and has thickened (about 1 more minute). Add asparagus and steak, stirring just until heated through (1 to 2 minutes). Serve with rice. Makes about 4 servings.

■ *Per serving: 422 calories, 33 g protein, 37 g carbohydrates, 14 g total fat (5 g saturated fat), 64 mg cholesterol, 430 mg sodium*

Flank Steak Southwestern Style

Preparation time: About 25 minutes

Cooking time: 15 to 20 minutes

Baking time: About 1¾ hours

A spicy tortilla filling and a green chile salsa used as cooking liquid give this rolled steak a Santa Fe flair. For added authenticity, use blue corn tortillas.

> 1 tablespoon salad oil
> 1 large onion, finely chopped
> 1 large tomato (about 8 oz.), seeded and chopped
> ½ teaspoon *each* dry oregano leaves and crushed dried hot red chiles
> ½ cup chopped cilantro (coriander)
> 3 corn tortillas, torn into bite-size strips
> ¼ cup sliced ripe olives
> 1 egg white
> 1½ pounds flank steak, trimmed of fat
>   Vegetable oil cooking spray
> 1 jar (12 oz.) green chile salsa
>   Cilantro (coriander) sprigs

Heat oil in a wide frying pan over medium heat. Add onion and cook, stirring often, until soft but not browned (about 5 minutes). Stir in tomato, oregano, and dried chiles. Continue to cook, stirring, until tomato is soft (6 to 8 minutes). Remove from heat and let cool for about 5 minutes. Stir in chopped cilantro, tortillas, olives, and egg white; set mixture aside.

Butterfly steak by slicing in half horizontally almost all the way through. Spread open; place on a board, cover with plastic wrap, and pound ¼ inch thick, using flat side of a meat mallet. Spoon tortilla mixture over half the steak; fold ends in. Starting with short side, roll to enclose. Tie securely with string at 1½-inch intervals.

Spray a wide nonstick frying pan with cooking spray; place over medium-high heat. Add steak and brown on all sides. Transfer to a 2- to 3-quart baking dish and pour salsa over steak. Cover and bake in a 375° oven until tender when pierced (about 1¾ hours); stir a little water into salsa, if needed. Remove string; cut steak roll into ¾-inch slices. Top with sauce and garnish with cilantro sprigs. Makes 6 servings.

■ *Per serving: 272 calories, 25 g protein, 15 g carbohydrates, 12 g total fat (4 g saturated fat), 57 mg cholesterol, 531 mg sodium*

Rich Brown Braised Beef

Preparation time: About 10 minutes

Cooking time: About 1 hour and 40 minutes

Without a separate browning step, morsels of beef simmer in minimal liquid to richly colored, tender succulence. Serve with noodles and a salad.

> 2 pounds boneless beef round tip, trimmed of fat
> 2 cloves garlic, minced or pressed
> 1 tablespoon salad oil
> 2 cups water
> 2 tablespoons *each* soy sauce, red wine vinegar, and grape jelly
> ¼ teaspoon *each* pepper, paprika, and dry oregano leaves
> 4 drops liquid hot pepper seasoning
> 1½ teaspoons cornstarch blended with 1 tablespoon cold water
>   Salt
>   Chopped parsley
> 1 pound egg noodles, cooked

Cut beef into 1-inch cubes. In a 3- to 3½-quart pan, combine beef, garlic, oil, and ½ cup of the water. Cover and simmer over medium heat for 30 minutes. Uncover and continue cooking, stirring often, until most of the juices have evaporated and browned (15 to 20 minutes). Stir in soy sauce, vinegar, jelly, pepper, paprika, oregano, hot pepper seasoning, and remaining 1½ cups water. Reduce heat, cover, and simmer until beef is very tender when pierced (about 45 minutes).

Gradually stir cornstarch mixture into cooking liquid. Increase heat to medium and cook, stirring occasionally, just until thickened (2 to 3 minutes). Season to taste with salt and garnish with parsley. Serve with noodles. Makes 8 servings.

■ *Per serving: 391 calories, 32 g protein, 45 g carbohydrates, 8 g total fat (2 g saturated fat), 122 mg cholesterol, 342 mg sodium*

Oven-browned meat cooks slowly with carrots, mushrooms and onions to make Easy Oven Beef Stew (recipe on facing page). Serve this hearty, lowfat entrée with crusty French bread.

■ *Pictured on facing page*

Easy Oven Beef Stew

Preparation time: About 20 minutes

Baking time: About 3 hours

Oven-browning is an unconventional but effective way to brown meat without adding extra fat. Tender beef and chunky vegetables cook slowly in the oven to create a flavorful main dish.

- 2 **pounds boneless beef round tip, trimmed of fat**
- 2 **to 3 tablespoons all-purpose flour**
- 1½ **cups water**
- 6 **medium-size carrots (about 1¼ lbs. *total*), sliced about 1 inch thick**
- ½ **pound small mushrooms or quartered large mushrooms**
- 2 **small red onions (about 6 oz. *total*), quartered lengthwise**
- ½ **cup finely chopped parsley**
  Salt

Cut beef into 1-inch cubes; coat with flour, shaking off excess. Arrange cubes slightly apart in an ungreased 9- by 13-inch baking dish or pan. Bake, uncovered, in a 500° oven for 20 minutes. Remove dish from oven and let cool for about 5 minutes; meanwhile, reduce oven temperature to 350°. Gradually add water to dish, stirring to loosen any browned bits.

Add carrots, mushrooms, onions, and all but 1 tablespoon of the parsley. Cover tightly. Bake until beef is very tender, stirring once or twice (about 2½ hours). Season to taste with salt and garnish with remaining parsley. Makes 8 servings.

■ *Per serving: 197 calories, 26 g protein, 12 g carbohydrates, 5 g total fat (2 g saturated fat), 68 mg cholesterol, 98 mg sodium*

Flemish Beef Stew

Preparation time: About 15 minutes

Cooking time: About 2 hours

Beef round tip simmers to tenderness with a generous measure of onions, dark beer, and herbs—a recipe based on the classic Belgian stew, *carbonnade*. Traditionally served with mashed potatoes, it's also good with lightly toasted sourdough bread and Brussels sprouts.

- 2 **pounds boneless beef round tip, trimmed of fat**
- 2 **bottles or cans (12 oz. *each*) dark beer, ale, or stout**
- 3 **large onions, thinly sliced**
- ½ **teaspoon pepper**
- 2 **tablespoons all-purpose flour**
- 1 **large clove garlic, minced or pressed**
- 1 **bay leaf**
- 1 **teaspoon dry thyme leaves**
- ⅓ **cup finely chopped parsley**
- 1½ **tablespoons red wine vinegar**
  Salt

Cut beef into 1½-inch chunks. In a wide 3½- to 4-quart pan, combine beef and ½ cup of the beer over medium heat; cover and simmer for 30 minutes. Add onions and pepper; cook, uncovered, stirring occasionally, until most of the liquid has evaporated and juices and onions are browned (30 to 35 minutes). Add flour and stir gently for 30 seconds. Gradually blend in remaining 2½ cups beer, stirring to loosen any browned bits. Mix in garlic, bay leaf, thyme, and all but about 1 tablespoon of the parsley.

Cover, reduce heat, and simmer until beef is very tender when pierced (about 1 more hour). Stir in vinegar and season to taste with salt. Garnish with remaining parsley. Makes 8 servings.

■ *Per serving: 186 calories, 25 g protein, 10 g carbohydrates, 4 g total fat (1 g saturated fat), 68 mg cholesterol, 77 mg sodium*

Lean Potatoes

Meat and potatoes traditionally have been natural partners, and still can be—it's all in the cooking techniques and seasonings. Potatoes are an excellent source of complex carbohydrates and vitamin C, so be sure to keep them in your menu plans.

Following are tasty lowfat potato dishes to team up with your lean-meat entrées.

Spicy Baked Potato Sticks

3   to 4 small russet potatoes (about 1½ lbs. *total*)
½   teaspoon ground cumin
⅛   teaspoon ground red pepper (cayenne)
    Olive oil cooking spray
    Salt

Scrub potatoes but do not peel; then quarter lengthwise. Mix cumin and red pepper. Spray a shallow rimmed baking pan with cooking spray. Place potatoes in pan, skin sides down, in a single layer; spray cut surfaces with additional cooking spray. Sprinkle with cumin mixture. Bake, uncovered, in a 400° oven until potatoes are golden brown and tender when pierced (about 1 hour). Season to taste with salt. Makes 4 servings.

■ *Per serving: 142 calories, 3 g protein, 31 g carbohydrates, 1 g total fat (0 g saturated fat), 0 mg cholesterol, 14 mg sodium*

Mustard-baked Potato Sticks. Scrub and cut potatoes as directed for Spicy Baked Potato Sticks. Omit cumin and ground red pepper. Combine 1

tablespoon *each* **vegetable oil** and **Dijon mustard** with 1 teaspoon **lemon juice.** Spray pan with cooking spray and arrange potatoes as directed; drizzle cut surfaces with mustard mixture. Bake as directed. Omit salt. Makes 4 servings.

■ *Per serving: 176 calories, 3 g protein, 31 g carbohydrates, 4 g total fat (.5 g saturated fat), 0 mg cholesterol, 126 mg sodium*

Garlic-roasted Potatoes & Greens

2   pounds thin-skinned potatoes
    Olive oil cooking spray
6   large cloves garlic, quartered
3   tablespoons red wine vinegar
1   tablespoon olive oil
    Salt and freshly ground pepper
3   to 4 cups watercress sprigs, rinsed and crisped

Scrub potatoes but do not peel; then cut into ¾-inch cubes (you should have about 6 cups). Spray a shallow rimmed baking pan with cooking spray. Mix potatoes and garlic in prepared pan; spray with cooking spray. Bake, uncovered, in a 450° oven until well browned, turning with a wide spatula at 15-minute intervals (about 1 hour *total*).

Drizzle vinegar and oil over potatoes. Turn potato mixture gently with spatula to loosen any browned bits. Season to taste with salt and pepper and transfer to a wide bowl. Coarsely chop about half the watercress; mix lightly with potatoes. Tuck remaining watercress around potatoes. Serve hot or at room temperature. Makes 4 to 6 servings.

■ *Per serving: 187 calories, 4 g protein, 35 g carbohydrates, 4 g total fat (.5 g saturated fat), 0 mg cholesterol, 25 mg sodium*

■ *Pictured on page 23*

Curried New Potatoes with Green Onions

    12 small thin-skinned potatoes, each 1½ to 2
        inches in diameter (about 1 lb. *total*)
    1½ tablespoons salad oil
    1   tablespoon mustard seeds, coarsely
        crushed
    1½ teaspoons curry powder
    ⅓   cup thinly sliced green onions (including
        tops)
        Salt

Scrub potatoes but do not peel. Steam, covered, on a
rack over about 1 inch of boiling water until tender
when pierced (about 25 minutes). Halve warm
potatoes.

Heat oil in a wide nonstick frying pan over
medium heat. Stir in mustard seeds and curry
powder; add potatoes, cut sides down. Cook until
lightly browned (about 5 minutes). Stir in green
onions and continue cooking for about 30 seconds.
Season to taste with salt. Makes 4 servings.

■ *Per serving: 155 calories, 3 g protein, 22 g carbohydrates, 6 g
total fat (1 g saturated fat), 0 mg cholesterol, 10 mg sodium*

Pesto–Orange Potato Salad

    2   pounds russet potatoes, cooked and
        peeled
    2   medium-size oranges
    ½   cup *each* lightly packed parsley and
        cilantro (coriander)
    ¼   cup grated Parmesan cheese
    ¾   cup plain lowfat yogurt
    1   teaspoon sugar
        Salt and pepper
    ½   cup walnut halves

Cut potatoes into ½-inch cubes and place in a large
bowl. Grate 2 teaspoons of peel from oranges and
set aside. Remove and discard remaining peel from
oranges. Over a small bowl, cut out orange segments, catching juice in bowl; set aside.

In a blender or food processor, combine orange
juice, grated orange peel, parsley, cilantro, cheese,
yogurt, and sugar; whirl until smooth. Pour yogurt
mixture over potatoes and mix gently. Season to taste
with salt and pepper. Garnish with orange segments
and walnuts. Makes 6 to 8 servings.

■ *Per serving: 203 calories, 6 g protein, 32 g carbohydrates, 6 g
total fat (1 g saturated fat), 4 mg cholesterol, 83 mg sodium*

Garlic Mashed Potatoes

    2   large heads garlic (about 6 oz. *total*)
        Olive oil cooking spray
    3   pounds russet potatoes, peeled and
        quartered
    ½   cup warm evaporated skim milk
    1   tablespoon margarine
        Salt and pepper

Place garlic in a small baking pan and coat with
cooking spray. Bake in a 450° oven until garlic is
very soft when squeezed (about 45 minutes); cool
slightly. Meanwhile, place potatoes in a 5- to 6-quart
pan with enough water to cover by 1 inch. Cover
and bring to a boil over high heat. Reduce heat and
continue boiling gently until potatoes are tender
when pierced (20 to 25 minutes); drain well.

While potatoes are cooking, cut garlic heads in half
crosswise and squeeze soft garlic from peel into a
large bowl. Beat garlic with an electric mixer until
smooth. Add hot potatoes, milk, and margarine. Beat
until smooth. Season to taste with salt and pepper.
Makes 6 to 8 servings.

■ *Per serving: 173 calories, 5 g protein, 34 g carbohydrates, 2 g
total fat (0 g saturated fat), 1 mg cholesterol, 54 mg sodium*

Baked Potatoes & Apples

    2   pounds small thin-skinned potatoes
    2   medium-size onions, cut into 1-inch
        wedges
    2   tablespoons olive oil
    1   pound tart red-skinned apples
    1¼ cups regular-strength beef broth
    ¾   cup apple juice
    2   tablespoons cornstarch
    ¾   teaspoon ground allspice

Scrub potatoes but do not peel; place in a 9- by 13-
inch baking pan. Break apart onion wedges and
sprinkle over potatoes. Add oil and mix well. Bake,
uncovered, in a 400° oven, stirring occasionally, for
25 minutes. Meanwhile, quarter and core apples; cut
into ¾-inch wedges. In a small bowl, combine beef
broth, apple juice, cornstarch, and allspice.

Add juice mixture and apples to potato mixture.
Continue baking, spooning on juices several times,
until potatoes are very tender when pierced and juices
begin to form thick bubbles (about 25 more minutes).
Makes 8 servings.

■ *Per serving: 181 calories, 3 g protein, 35 g carbohydrates, 4 g
total fat (.5 g saturated fat), 0 mg cholesterol, 139 mg sodium*

Herb & Spice Simmered Beef

Preparation time: About 15 minutes

Baking time: 2½ to 3 hours

After browning, transfer this roast to a deep pan or covered casserole and oven-braise in a rich, spicy wine sauce. During the last hour of cooking, bake potatoes in the oven alongside the simmering beef.

Vegetable oil cooking spray

1 **boneless beef round tip roast (about 3 lbs.), trimmed of fat**

1 **large onion, thinly sliced**

2 **cups regular-strength beef broth**

¾ **cup dry red wine**

3 **tablespoons *each* catsup and cider vinegar**

2 **bay leaves**

1 **teaspoon dry thyme leaves**

5 ***each* whole cloves and whole allspice**

10 **to 12 russet potatoes (about 8 oz. *each*)**

2 **tablespoons cornstarch blended with 2 tablespoons water**

Salt and pepper

Coat a wide nonstick frying pan with cooking spray. Add roast and brown on all sides over medium-high heat. Transfer to a 3- to 4-quart ovenproof pan or deep casserole; set aside. In frying pan, combine onion, beef broth, wine, catsup, vinegar, bay leaves, thyme, cloves, and allspice; bring to a boil. Pour mixture over meat and cover. Bake in a 325° oven until meat is very tender, turning once or twice (2½ to 3 hours). About an hour before roast is done, scrub potatoes well and pierce each in several places with a fork. Place in oven around pan.

Transfer roast and potatoes to a warm, deep platter and cover lightly to keep warm. Skim and discard fat, if necessary, from cooking liquid. Discard bay leaves. Using a wire whisk, stir cornstarch mixture into liquid. Cook over high heat, stirring, until sauce is boiling and has thickened (about 1 minute). Season to taste with salt and pepper. Slice roast thinly and serve with sauce and potatoes. Makes 10 to 12 servings.

■ *Per serving: 360 calories, 31 g protein, 45 g carbohydrates, 5 g total fat (2 g saturated fat), 74 mg cholesterol, 294 mg sodium*

■ *Pictured on facing page*

Oven-braised Beef in Red Wine

Preparation time: About 20 minutes

Baking time: 2½ to 3 hours

Vegetables and meat drippings enrich and thicken the rich, dark, winy sauce which bastes this simmered roast. Serve the beef with linguine or other pasta.

Vegetable oil cooking spray

1 **boneless beef round tip roast (about 3 lbs.), trimmed of fat**

Coarsely ground pepper

1 **large onion, chopped**

2 **cloves garlic, minced or pressed**

1 **medium-size carrot (about 3 oz.), coarsely shredded**

1 **stalk celery, chopped**

6 **whole cloves**

1½ **cups dry red wine**

1 **tablespoon tomato paste**

½ **teaspoon *each* salt and dry thyme leaves**

¼ **cup rum (optional)**

Italian parsley sprigs

Coat a wide nonstick frying pan with cooking spray. Add roast and brown on all sides over medium-high heat. Transfer to a 3- to 4-quart ovenproof pan or deep casserole; season to taste with pepper. Set aside. In frying pan, combine onion, garlic, carrot, celery, cloves, wine, tomato paste, salt, and thyme; bring to a boil. Pour mixture over meat and cover. Bake in a 350° oven until meat is very tender, turning once or twice (2½ to 3 hours).

Lift out roast and place on a warm, deep platter; cover lightly to keep warm. Skim and discard fat, if necessary, from cooking liquid; then pour into a blender or food processor. Whirl until puréed. Pour into a 2-quart pan, add rum, if desired, and bring to a boil over high heat. Add water, if needed, to make about 1¾ cups. Slice roast thinly and serve with sauce; garnish with parsley. Makes 10 to 12 servings.

■ *Per serving: 168 calories, 27 g protein, 3 g carbohydrates, 5 g total fat (2 g saturated fat), 74 mg cholesterol, 196 mg sodium*

*Baked to tender perfection, Oven-braised Beef in Red Wine
(recipe on facing page) shares platter with graceful strands of tricolor
linguine; ladle rich red-brown sauce over thinly sliced meat. Serve with
green salad, breadsticks, and hearty red wine.*

31

Pot Roast with Pineapple Rice

Preparation time: About 15 minutes

Cooking time: About 2½ hours

Tropical flavors permeate this beef round tip roast as it simmers. Fluffy rice, flavored with fresh pineapple and finely chopped candied ginger, complements the meat.

- 1½ **tablespoons salad oil**
- 1 **boneless beef round tip roast (about 2½ lbs.), trimmed of fat**
- ¼ **cup soy sauce**
- 2 **cups water**
- 2 **cloves garlic, minced or pressed**
- ¼ **cup firmly packed brown sugar**
- 2 **tablespoons finely chopped preserved or candied ginger**
- ¼ **cup finely chopped onion**
- 1 **cup short-grain (pearl) rice**
- ½ **cup pineapple juice**
- 2 **teaspoons cornstarch blended with 1 tablespoon cold water**
- 1 **cup diced fresh pineapple**
  Slivered green onions (including tops)

Heat ½ tablespoon of the oil in a deep, heavy 3½- to 4-quart pan over medium-high heat. Add roast and brown on all sides. Add soy sauce, ½ cup of the water, garlic, sugar, and half the ginger. Reduce heat, cover, and simmer, turning roast in liquid once or twice, until very tender when pierced (about 2½ hours).

About 30 minutes before meat is done, heat remaining tablespoon of the oil in a wide frying pan over medium heat. Add chopped onion and rice; cook, stirring often, until rice is opaque (about 3 minutes). Add pineapple juice and remaining 1½ cups water. Reduce heat, cover, and simmer until rice is just tender and liquid has been absorbed (20 to 25 minutes).

Meanwhile, remove roast to a warm, deep platter and cover lightly to keep warm. Skim and discard fat, if necessary, from cooking liquid; then stir in cornstarch mixture. Increase heat to medium-high and cook, stirring, until sauce is bubbling and has thickened.

Just before serving, lightly mix pineapple and remaining tablespoon of ginger into rice. Slice roast thinly and serve with rice and sauce. Garnish with green onions. Makes 8 to 10 servings.

■ *Per serving: 316 calories, 29 g protein, 32 g carbohydrates, 7 g total fat (2 g saturated fat), 540 mg sodium*

Portuguese Roast Beef

Preparation time: About 10 minutes

Marinating time: At least 8 hours

Roasting time: 2½ to 3 hours

This Portuguese method of cooking beef produces a tender oven roast from a very lean cut. Part of the secret is a piquant chile and vinegar marinade. Potatoes are precooked in some of the marinade, then brown with the meat.

- 2 **cups** *each* **cider vinegar and water**
- 6 **cloves garlic, minced or pressed**
- 1 **teaspoon** *each* **sugar, salt, and dry basil leaves**
- 2 **bay leaves**
- 1 **or 2 small dried hot red chiles, crushed**
- 1 **boneless beef round tip roast (about 3 lbs.), trimmed of fat**
  About 2 tablespoons all-purpose flour
- 2 **to 2½ pounds small thin-skinned potatoes, peeled if desired**
- 1¼ **cups water**
- 2 **tablespoons all-purpose flour blended with 3 tablespoons cold water**

Continued on next page

In a large bowl, combine vinegar, the 2 cups water, garlic, sugar, salt, basil, bay leaves, and chiles. Add roast, cover, and refrigerate for at least 8 hours or until next day.

Lift roast from bowl, reserving marinade. Pat meat dry and dust with flour. Place on a lightly greased rack in a roasting pan. Roast, uncovered, in a 325° oven for 1½ hours. After about 1 hour, place potatoes in a 3- to 4-quart pan in about 1 inch of the marinade. Cook over medium-high heat until barely tender when pierced (20 to 25 minutes).

Remove roasting pan from oven, set rack aside, and place roast directly in pan. Lift potatoes from cooking liquid and arrange around meat, turning to coat with pan juices. Return to oven and roast, turning potatoes once and basting meat and potatoes several times with marinade, until meat is very tender when pierced (1 to 1½ hours).

Transfer roast and potatoes to a warm, deep platter and cover lightly to keep warm. Gradually add the 1¼ cups water and ¼ cup of the marinade to roasting pan, stirring to loosen any browned bits. Pour liquid into a 2-quart pan and blend in flour mixture. Cook over medium-high heat, stirring constantly, until gravy is bubbling and has thickened. Slice roast thinly. Serve with potatoes and pass gravy to spoon over individual portions. Makes 10 to 12 servings.

■ *Per serving: 243 calories, 28 g protein, 20 g carbohydrates, 5 g total fat (2 g saturated fat), 74 mg cholesterol, 145 mg sodium*

■ *Pictured on front cover*

Citrus-seasoned Steak & Brown Rice

Preparation time: About 10 minutes

Marinating time: At least 3 hours

Cooking time: About 1 hour

Broiling time: 20 to 25 minutes

This recipe calls for a thick slice of top round (sometimes labeled "London broil"). Orange juice and aromatic orange peel add a tangy accent to this pairing of rare beef and herbed brown rice.

> 1 orange
> 2½ pounds boneless beef top round (1½ to 2 inches thick), trimmed of fat
> ½ teaspoon dry thyme leaves
> ¼ cup white wine vinegar
> 1 tablespoon salad oil
>   Brown Rice à l'Orange (recipe follows)
>   Salt
>   Orange slices
>   Raspberries (optional)
>   Sage sprigs

Grate 1 teaspoon of peel from orange; cut 3 thin strips of peel (*each* about 2 inches long). Set aside to use in Brown Rice à l'Orange. Squeeze orange to obtain ⅓ cup juice. Place beef in a shallow bowl with grated peel, thyme, vinegar, oil, and 3 tablespoons of the orange juice; turn beef to coat. Cover and refrigerate for at least 3 hours or until next day.

About 30 minutes before broiling beef, prepare Brown Rice à l'Orange. Lift beef from bowl, reserving marinade. Place beef on rack of a broiler pan. Broil about 6 inches below heat, basting occasionally with marinade and turning once, until well browned and a meat thermometer registers 120° to 125° for rare to medium-rare (20 to 25 minutes *total*).

Transfer beef to a carving board and cover lightly to keep warm. Skim and discard fat, if necessary, from pan drippings. Add remaining orange juice and cook, stirring, over medium heat until blended. Season pan juices and beef to taste with salt. Slice beef thinly across grain at a slant. Garnish with orange slices, raspberries, if desired, and sage. Serve with Brown Rice à l'Orange and offer pan juices to spoon over individual portions. Makes 8 to 10 servings.

Brown Rice à l'Orange. In a 3- to 3½-quart pan, combine 2 cups **orange juice,** 1 cup *each* **water** and **dry white wine,** 5 sprigs **sage** (or ½ teaspoon dry sage leaves), and 3 thin strips **orange peel** (*each* about 2 inches long). Bring to a boil over high heat; stir in 2 cups **long-grain brown rice.** Cover, reduce heat, and simmer until rice is tender (55 to 60 minutes). Remove from heat; let stand, uncovered, for 5 minutes. Discard orange peel and sage sprigs; fluff rice with a fork.

■ *Per serving: 227 calories, 30 g protein, 14 g carbohydrates, 5 g total fat (2 g saturated fat), 72 mg cholesterol, 67 mg sodium*

*Green onions share the barbecue with Grilled Beef with
Soy-seasoned Sake (recipe on facing page). Accompany with colorful vegetables
steamed tender-crisp, and pour a foamy glass of your favorite beer to
complete this breezy summer dinner.*

■ Pictured on facing page

Grilled Beef with Soy-seasoned Sake

Preparation time: About 15 minutes

Grilling time: 20 to 25 minutes

Both this thick, boneless steak and the green onion sauce cook on the barbecue. For the tangy sauce, use a sturdy, metal-handled frying pan.

- 1½ **pounds boneless beef top round (about 2 inches thick), trimmed of fat**
- 1 **tablespoon Oriental sesame oil or salad oil**
- 2 **cloves garlic, minced or pressed**
- 2 **tablespoons grated fresh ginger**
- ½ **cup thinly sliced green onions (including tops)**
- ⅔ **cup sake or dry sherry**
- 3 **tablespoons soy sauce**
- 12 **green onions, ends trimmed**
  Salt and pepper

Place beef on a lightly greased grill 4 to 6 inches above a solid bed of medium-hot coals. Cook, turning once, until beef is browned and a meat thermometer inserted in thickest part registers 135° to 140° for rare to medium-rare (20 to 25 minutes *total*).

Meanwhile, in a metal-handled 6- to 8-inch frying pan, combine oil, garlic, ginger, and sliced green onions; place on grill over coals. Cook, stirring often, until onions are limp (5 to 8 minutes). Add sake and soy sauce. Continue cooking, stirring once or twice, until mixture boils; then move to a cooler part of the grill.

When beef is almost done, lay whole green onions on grill and cook, turning once, until lightly browned (2 to 4 minutes *total*). Transfer beef and whole onions to a serving board; slice beef thinly across grain. Top with warm green onion sauce. Season to taste with salt and pepper. Makes 6 servings.

■ *Per serving: 232 calories, 28 g protein, 7 g carbohydrates, 7 g total fat (2 g saturated fat), 72 mg cholesterol, 571 mg sodium*

Rippled Beef Teriyaki with Pickled Maui Onions

Preparation time: About 20 minutes

Marinating time: At least 2 hours for beef; at least 3 days for onions

Grilling time: 4 to 6 minutes

Strips of teriyaki-marinated beef, pounded thin and rippled onto skewers, make an appealing summer dish. Team them with sweet and sour onions, rice, and sliced pineapple or papaya heated on the grill.

Pickled Maui Onions (recipe follows)
- 1½ **pounds boneless beef top round (about ¾ inch thick), trimmed of fat**
- ⅓ **cup soy sauce**
- 2 **tablespoons sugar**
- 1 **tablespoon grated fresh ginger**
- 2 **cloves garlic, minced or pressed**
- 2 **tablespoons sake or dry sherry**
- 1 **teaspoon Oriental sesame oil**

Prepare Pickled Maui Onions.

Cut beef in half lengthwise. Place each half between sheets of plastic wrap and pound with flat side of a meat mallet until about ¼ inch thick. Cut into 2-inch-wide strips. In a shallow bowl, combine soy

sauce, sugar, ginger, garlic, sake, and oil; stir until sugar is dissolved. Add beef. Cover and refrigerate for at least 2 hours or until next day.

Lift meat from bowl, reserving marinade. Weave meat, ripple-fashion, onto long, thin skewers. Place on a lightly greased grill 4 to 6 inches above a solid bed of medium-hot coals. Cook, turning skewers once and brushing meat with marinade, until browned (4 to 6 minutes *total* for rare to medium-rare). Serve with Pickled Maui Onions. Makes 6 servings.

■ *Per serving: 176 calories, 28 g protein, 4 g carbohydrates, 5 g total fat (2 g saturated fat), 72 mg cholesterol, 601 mg sodium*

Pickled Maui Onions. Cut 1 large **Maui onion** or other mild white onion lengthwise into 1-inch-wide chunks. Place in a wide-mouth, 3- to 4-cup heatproof jar. In a 1- to 1½-quart pan, combine ¾ cup **water;** 6 tablespoons **distilled white vinegar;** 3 tablespoons **sugar;** 2 cloves **garlic,** crushed; 1 **small dried hot red chile;** and 1½ teaspoons **salt.** Bring to a boil over high heat, stirring until sugar is dissolved. Pour hot liquid over onions; cover tightly. Let cool; then refrigerate for at least 3 days or up to 1 month.

■ *Per serving: 41 calories, 1 g protein, 10 g carbohydrates, 0 g total fat (0 g saturated fat), 0 mg cholesterol, 550 mg sodium*

Hungarian Beef Stew

Preparation time: About 20 minutes

Cooking time: About 2 hours

Small whole mushrooms and chopped leeks distinguish this simmered stew. Its Hungarian character derives from red bell pepper and a spoonful of paprika. Serve it with wide egg noodles.

1½ **pounds boneless beef top round, trimmed of fat**
1 **can (14½ oz.) regular-strength beef broth**
1 **clove garlic, minced or pressed**
1 **tablespoon sweet Hungarian paprika**
1 **bunch leeks (3 or 4 medium-size)**
1 **large red bell pepper (8 to 10 oz.), seeded and cut into 1-inch squares**
½ **pound small mushrooms (about 1-inch diameter)**
½ **teaspoon salt**
¼ **teaspoon pepper**
2 **tablespoons port or Madeira**
½ **cup plain lowfat yogurt blended with 1 tablespoon cornstarch**

Cut beef into 1-inch cubes. In a wide 3½- to 4-quart pan, combine beef and ½ cup of the beef broth over medium heat. Cover and simmer for 30 minutes. Add garlic and paprika; continue cooking, uncovered, stirring occasionally, until most of the liquid has evaporated and juices are browned (about 30 minutes).

Meanwhile, cut off and discard all but 1½ inches of green tops from leeks. Split leeks lengthwise, rinse well, and cut into 1-inch lengths; set aside. Blend remaining 1¼ cups beef broth into stew, stirring to loosen any browned bits. Mix in leeks, bell pepper, mushrooms, salt, and pepper.

Cover, reduce heat, and simmer until beef is very tender when pierced (about 1 more hour). Stir in port and yogurt mixture. Increase heat to medium-high and bring to a boil, stirring, until stew is bubbling and has thickened (2 to 3 minutes). Makes 6 servings.

■ *Per serving: 216 calories, 29 g protein, 12 g carbohydrates, 5 g total fat (2 g saturated fat), 66 mg cholesterol, 514 mg sodium*

Beef & Olive Stew

Preparation time: About 10 minutes

Cooking time: About 2½ hours

This aromatic stew simmers slowly while you prepare the rest of the meal. Serve it with couscous, cooked in beef or chicken broth, and a green salad.

2 **pounds boneless beef top round, trimmed of fat**
1 **tablespoon soy sauce**
1 **cup water**
1 **large onion, chopped**
1 **clove garlic, minced or pressed**
2 **tablespoons minced fresh ginger or ½ teaspoon ground ginger**
1 **cup dry red wine**
1 **can (15 oz.) tomato purée**
1 **teaspoon dry sage leaves**
¼ **teaspoon pepper**
½ **cup Niçoise or small ripe olives**
Salt

Cut beef into 1-inch cubes. In a wide 3½- to 4-quart pan, combine beef, soy sauce, and ½ cup of the water over medium heat. Cover and simmer for 30 minutes. Add onion, garlic, and ginger; cook, uncovered, stirring occasionally, until most of the liquid has evaporated and onions are browned (25 to 30 minutes). Blend in remaining ½ cup water, stirring to loosen any browned bits.

Mix in wine, tomato purée, sage, and pepper. Cover, reduce heat, and simmer until beef is almost tender when pierced (about 1 hour). Stir in olives; continue cooking, covered, until beef is very tender when pierced (about 30 more minutes). Season to taste with salt. Makes 8 servings.

■ *Per serving: 188 calories, 27 g protein, 8 g carbohydrates, 5 g total fat (1 g saturated fat), 65 mg cholesterol, 475 mg sodium*

Beef & Pork Chili with Beer

Preparation time: About 30 minutes

Cooking time: 2 to 2½ hours

A little pork gives this beef chili extra flavor. Other additions to the savory blend include a can of beer, green chile salsa, cilantro, and a fresh jalapeño.

- 1½ **pounds boneless beef top round, trimmed of fat**
- ½ **pound lean boneless pork (from leg or loin), trimmed of fat**
- 1 **bottle or can (12 oz.) beer**
- 2 **medium-size onions, chopped**
- 2 **cloves garlic, minced or pressed**
- ¼ **cup masa flour (corn tortilla flour)**
- 1 **large can (28 oz.) tomatoes**
- 2 **tablespoons chili powder**
- 1 **teaspoon *each* ground cumin and dry oregano leaves**
- ½ **cup chopped cilantro (coriander)**
- 1 **can (7 oz.) green chile salsa**
- 1 **medium-size fresh jalapeño chile, seeded and finely chopped**
- 1 **large green bell pepper, seeded and finely chopped**
- 2 **tablespoons lime or lemon juice**
  Salt
  Garnishes (optional; suggestions follow)

Cut beef and pork into 1-inch cubes. In a wide 3½- to 4-quart pan, combine beef, pork, and ½ cup of the beer over medium heat. Cover and simmer for 30 minutes.

Add onions and garlic; cook, uncovered, stirring occasionally, until most of the liquid has evaporated and juices and onions are browned (30 to 35 minutes). Add masa and stir gently for 30 seconds. Gradually blend in remaining 1 cup beer, stirring to loosen any browned bits. Mix in tomatoes (break up with a spoon) and their liquid, chili powder, cumin, oregano, cilantro, salsa, jalapeño, and bell pepper. Cover, reduce heat, and simmer until beef is very tender when pierced (1 to 1½ hours more). Stir in lime juice and season to taste with salt. Offer garnishes to sprinkle over individual portions, if desired. Makes 8 servings.

Garnishes. In separate bowls, offer 1 medium-size **avocado**, peeled, seeded, and chopped; ½ cup sliced **green onions** (including tops); **lime** wedges; and 1 cup (4 oz.) shredded **jack cheese.**

■ *Per serving: 214 calories, 27 g protein, 14 g carbohydrates, 5 g total fat (2 g saturated fat), 68 mg cholesterol, 403 mg sodium*

Baked Beef Stew with Carrots

Preparation time: About 25 minutes

Baking time: 2¼ to 2¾ hours

This hearty oven stew takes time to cook but needs little attention. Freshly mashed potatoes make a nice accompaniment.

- 2 **pounds boneless beef top round, trimmed of fat**
- 2 **medium-size onions, thinly sliced**
- 1 **tablespoon all-purpose flour**
- 1 **can (14½ oz.) regular-strength beef broth**
- ¼ **cup red wine vinegar**
- 1 **teaspoon *each* dry thyme leaves and dry rosemary**
- ½ **teaspoon pepper**
- 1½ **pounds medium-size carrots, sliced ¼-inch thick (about 4 cups)**
  Salt

Cut beef into ¾-inch by 2-inch strips. In a shallow 3- to 3½-quart casserole, combine beef and onions. Bake, uncovered, in a 450° oven, stirring occasionally, until beef and onions are browned (40 to 45 minutes). Remove from oven; sprinkle with flour and stir gently to coat. Reduce oven temperature to 350°.

In a 1½-quart pan, combine beef broth, vinegar, thyme, rosemary, and pepper; bring to a boil over high heat. Add to beef mixture, stirring to loosen any browned bits. Distribute carrots over beef. Cover tightly and bake until beef is very tender when pierced (1½ to 2 hours). Season to taste with salt. Makes 8 servings.

■ *Per serving: 198 calories, 28 g protein, 12 g carbohydrates, 4 g total fat (1 g saturated fat), 65 mg cholesterol, 277 mg sodium*

■ Pictured on facing page

Eye of Round in Caper Sauce

Preparation time: About 10 minutes

Cooking time: 2 to 3 minutes

These fine-grained steaks are pounded to tender thinness, quickly sautéed, and drizzled with a sauce of mustard, capers, and lemon.

> 4 **beef eye of round steaks,** *each* **about ½ inch thick (1 lb.** *total***), trimmed of fat**
>
> **About 1 tablespoon all-purpose flour**
>
> **Olive oil cooking spray**
>
> 1 **teaspoon margarine**
>
> 1 **teaspoon** *each* **Dijon mustard and drained capers**
>
> 1 **tablespoon** *each* **lemon juice and chopped chives**

Place steaks between sheets of plastic wrap and pound with flat side of a meat mallet until about ¼ inch thick. Dust with flour, shaking off excess.

Spray a wide nonstick frying pan with cooking spray and place over medium-high heat. Cook steaks, turning once, until browned on both sides (2 to 3 minutes *total*). Transfer steaks to plates and keep warm.

Remove pan from heat and add margarine; stir in mustard, capers, and lemon juice. Drizzle caper sauce over steaks; garnish with chives. Makes 4 servings.

■ *Per serving: 170 calories, 25 g protein, 2 g carbohydrates, 6 g total fat (2 g saturated fat), 61 mg cholesterol, 128 mg sodium*

Marinated Daube of Beef

Preparation time: About 30 minutes

Marinating time: At least 8 hours

Cooking time: About 2¾ hours

In this lowfat version of the classic wine-marinated French stew, beef cubes are browned and cooked by sweating—a technique that uses very little fat. Vegetables add richness to the sauce; olives and orange peel provide unusual flavor accents.

> 2 **pounds beef eye of round, trimmed of fat**
>
> 1 **cup dry red wine**
>
> 2 **teaspoons olive oil**
>
> ¼ **cup chopped parsley**
>
> 1 **bay leaf**
>
> ½ **teaspoon dry thyme**
>
> ¼ **teaspoon white pepper**
>
> 2 **strips orange peel,** *each* **about ½ inch by 3 inches**
>
> 2 **medium-size onions, thinly sliced**
>
> 1½ **cups water**
>
> 1 **clove garlic, minced or pressed**
>
> 4 **medium-size carrots (about 12 oz.** *total***), sliced diagonally ¼ inch thick**
>
> 3 **medium-size tomatoes (about 1 lb.** *total***), peeled and cut into thin wedges**
>
> ½ **pound mushrooms, quartered**
>
> ⅓ **cup whole Niçoise or pitted ripe olives**
>
> 1 **tablespoon cornstarch blended with 2 tablespoons cold water**
>
> **Salt**
>
> 12 **small thin-skinned potatoes, steamed or baked**

Cut beef into 1-inch cubes. In a 2- to 3-quart bowl, combine beef, wine, oil, parsley, bay leaf, thyme, pepper, and orange peel. Cover and refrigerate for at least 8 hours.

Lift beef from bowl, reserving marinade. In a heavy 3½- to 4-quart pan, combine beef, onions, ½ cup of the water, and garlic over low heat. Cover and simmer, stirring occasionally, for 30 minutes. Uncover, increase heat to medium, and cook, stirring often, until most of the juices have evaporated and browned (about 25 minutes). Stir in reserved marinade and remaining 1 cup water; reduce heat, cover, and simmer for 45 minutes.

Stir in carrots and tomatoes; cover and continue cooking for 30 minutes. Add mushrooms and olives; cover and continue cooking until beef is very tender when pierced (30 to 45 minutes). Blend in cornstarch mixture; increase heat to medium-high and cook, stirring, until liquid is bubbling and has thickened. Season to taste with salt. Serve with potatoes. Makes 8 servings.

■ *Per serving: 285 calories, 28 g protein, 27 g carbohydrates, 7 g total fat (2 g saturated fat), 61 mg cholesterol, 138 mg sodium*

*When speedy preparation is important, Eye of Round in Caper Sauce
(recipe on facing page) goes together in minutes. Steaks are pounded thin to
tenderize before cooking, then are quickly sautéed. Add capers and other
seasonings to meat juices to create the flavorful sauce.*

Pot-roasted Eye of Round with Pasta

Preparation time: About 20 minutes

Cooking time: About 3½ hours

While this lean roast cooks, a delicious vegetable and anchovy sauce forms around it.

Vegetable oil cooking spray

1 beef eye of round roast (2½ to 3 lbs.), trimmed of fat

2 medium-size carrots (about 4 oz. *total*), chopped

1 large onion, finely chopped

2 stalks celery, finely chopped

2 cloves garlic, minced or pressed

1 can (14½ oz.) regular-strength beef broth

1 cup dry red wine

1 can (6 oz.) tomato paste

6 canned anchovy fillets, drained and finely chopped

1 bay leaf

½ pound mushrooms, quartered

1 pound dry corkscrew-shaped pasta (cavatappi)

Chopped Italian parsley

Coat a wide 3½- to 4-quart pan with cooking spray. Add roast and brown on all sides over medium-high heat. Surround with carrots, onion, celery, and garlic; pour in about ¼ cup of the beef broth and cook, stirring often, until onion begins to brown (about 5 minutes).

Stir in remaining beef broth, wine, tomato paste, anchovies, and bay leaf; bring to a boil. Reduce heat, cover, and simmer, turning beef once or twice, until nearly tender (about 2½ hours). Add mushrooms and continue cooking, uncovered, until beef is very tender when pierced (30 to 45 more minutes).

Meanwhile, in a 6- to 8-quart pan, cook pasta in 4 quarts boiling water just until tender (8 to 10 minutes); or cook according to package directions. Drain and transfer to a warm, deep platter. Slice beef thinly across grain. Arrange over pasta and spoon on some of the sauce. Garnish with parsley and serve with remaining sauce. Makes 8 servings.

■ *Per serving: 419 calories, 43 g protein, 41 g carbohydrates, 8 g total fat (2 g saturated fat), 86 mg cholesterol, 568 mg sodium*

Sauerbraten-style Eye of Round

Preparation time: About 15 minutes

Marinating time: At least 8 hours

Cooking time: About 3 hours

As this German-style pot roast cooks, the tart-sweet marinade becomes a gingersnap-thickened sauce.

½ cup catsup

1½ cups water

2 tablespoons *each* sugar and cider vinegar

1 tablespoon *each* prepared horseradish and Worcestershire

2 teaspoons dry mustard

½ teaspoon *each* salt and ground allspice

¼ teaspoon pepper

1 large onion, chopped

1 bay leaf

1 beef eye of round roast (1½ to 2 lbs.), trimmed of fat

⅓ cup crushed gingersnaps

3 to 4 cups cooked egg noodles

Chopped parsley

In a deep bowl, stir together catsup, ½ cup of the water, sugar, vinegar, horseradish, Worcestershire, mustard, salt, allspice, pepper, onion, and bay leaf. Add roast, turning to coat. Cover and refrigerate for at least 8 hours or until next day.

Transfer roast and marinade to a heavy 3½- to 4-quart pan; stir in remaining 1 cup water. Bring liquid to a boil over medium heat. Reduce heat, cover, and simmer, turning roast occasionally, until meat is very tender when pierced (about 3 hours). Transfer meat to a deep platter and cover lightly to keep warm. Skim and discard fat, if necessary, from cooking liquid. Stir in gingersnaps and bring to a boil over medium-high heat; cook, stirring, until crumbs are dissolved and sauce has thickened.

Slice roast thinly across grain and surround with noodles. Spoon on some of the sauce, then garnish with parsley. Pass remaining sauce at the table. Makes 6 to 8 servings.

■ *Per serving: 325 calories, 30 g protein, 35 g carbohydrates, 7 g total fat (2 g saturated fat), 90 mg cholesterol, 478 mg sodium*

Korean Braised Eye of Round

Preparation time: About 15 minutes

Cooking time: About 3 hours

Based on a Korean specialty, this braised beef roast cooks until tender in a flavorful broth of soy, garlic, sesame, and ginger that's thickened into a rich sauce before serving.

- 2 tablespoons sesame seeds
- 1½ cups water
- ¼ cup soy sauce
- 2 tablespoons sugar
- 2 cloves garlic, minced or pressed
- 3 thin slices fresh ginger
- 1 beef eye of round roast (about 1½ lbs.), trimmed of fat
- 2 large carrots (about 8 oz. *total*), sliced diagonally ¼ inch thick
- 1 teaspoon Oriental sesame oil
- 1 tablespoon cornstarch blended with 2 tablespoons cold water
- ¼ cup thinly sliced green onions (including tops)
- 3 cups hot cooked rice

In a heavy 3½- to 4-quart pan, stir sesame seeds over medium heat until golden (3 to 5 minutes). Remove pan from heat. Add water, soy sauce, sugar, garlic, and ginger; stir until sugar is dissolved. Add roast. Return pan to heat, increase heat to medium-high, and bring to a boil; cover, reduce heat, and simmer, turning roast occasionally, until beef is very tender when pierced (2½ to 3 hours).

Add carrots to pan with roast, cover, and continue cooking until carrots are tender (about 20 minutes). Transfer beef to a warm, deep platter; surround with carrots and cover platter lightly to keep warm. Stir oil and cornstarch mixture into liquid in pan; increase heat to medium-high and cook, stirring, until sauce is bubbling and has thickened. Slice beef thinly across grain. Spoon some of the sauce over beef and carrots; garnish with green onions. Serve with rice and pass remaining sauce to spoon over individual portions. Makes 6 servings.

■ *Per serving: 353 calories, 29 g protein, 40 g carbohydrates, 7 g total fat (2 g saturated fat), 61 mg cholesterol, 762 mg sodium*

Soy-braised Round Steak

Preparation time: About 15 minutes

Cooking time: 8 to 10 minutes

Baking time: 1 to 1½ hours

Slow, gentle cooking is recommended for this less tender portion of the round; the soy- and ginger-laced sauce is reminiscent of teriyaki. Serve with fluffy rice.

- 1 pound boneless beef bottom round steak (about ½ inch thick), trimmed of fat
- About 3 tablespoons all-purpose flour
- About ¼ cup evaporated skim milk
- 1 tablespoon salad oil
- 1 medium-size onion, thinly sliced
- ¼ cup soy sauce
- ½ cup regular-strength beef broth
- 1 tablespoon grated fresh ginger or ¾ teaspoon ground ginger
- About 2 tablespoons sliced green onions (including tops)

Cut beef into 4 portions; dust each with flour, shaking off excess. Dip into milk, then coat again with flour. Heat oil in a wide nonstick frying pan over medium-high heat. Add beef and brown on both sides, turning once. Add onion when beef is turned. Transfer beef to a shallow 2½- to 3-quart casserole. To pan, add soy sauce, beef broth, and ginger; stir into drippings and bring to a boil. Spoon soy mixture over beef. Cover and bake in a 325° oven until beef is very tender when pierced (1 to 1½ hours). Garnish with green onions. Makes 4 servings.

■ *Per serving: 248 calories, 28 g protein, 10 g carbohydrates, 10 g total fat (3 g saturated fat), 68 mg cholesterol, 1,218 mg sodium*

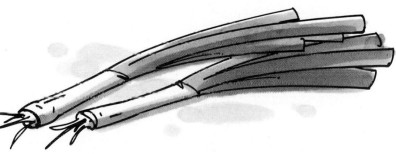

*Crumbled feta cheese accents cinnamon-scented Greek Beef Stew with
Onions (recipe on facing page), delicious spooned over tiny rice-shaped pasta.
Accompany with a sesame-sprinkled loaf of bread and fruity Greek olives.*

■ *Pictured on facing page*

Greek Beef Stew with Onions

Preparation time: About 25 minutes

Cooking time: About 2½ hours

This robust dish is based on the Greek *stifaido.* Serve with tiny rice-shaped pasta called orzo or seme di melone.

    2 pounds boneless beef bottom round, trimmed of fat
    1 tablespoon olive oil
 1½ cups water
    3 medium-size onions, finely chopped
    2 cloves garlic, minced or pressed
   ¼ teaspoon pepper
    1 bay leaf
    1 teaspoon sugar
   ½ teaspoon dry thyme leaves
    1 cinnamon stick (about 3 inches long)
    1 can (8 oz.) tomato sauce
   ½ cup dry red wine
    1 tablespoon red wine vinegar
      Salt
      Chopped parsley
  ⅓ to ½ cup crumbled feta cheese (optional)

Cut beef into 1-inch cubes. In a wide 3½- to 4-quart pan, combine beef, oil, and ½ cup of the water over medium heat. Cover and simmer for 30 minutes. Add onions, garlic, and pepper; cook, uncovered, stirring occasionally, until most of the liquid has evaporated and juices and onions are browned (30 to 35 minutes).

Blend in remaining cup water; add bay leaf, sugar, thyme, cinnamon stick, tomato sauce, and wine. Cover, reduce heat, and simmer until beef is very tender when pierced (about 1½ hours). Stir in vinegar and season to taste with salt. Garnish with parsley and, if desired, feta cheese. Makes 8 servings.

■ *Per serving: 203 calories, 26 g protein, 6 g carbohydrates, 8 g total fat (2 g saturated fat), 67 mg cholesterol, 240 mg sodium*

■ *Pictured on page 7*

Brandied Dijon Beef Stew

Preparation time: About 30 minutes

Cooking time: 2½ to 3 hours

Brandy and coarsely ground Dijon mustard add flavor to this French country stew. Complement it with small, whole vegetables—chive-sprinkled new potatoes and young green beans.

    2 pounds boneless beef bottom round, trimmed of fat
  ⅓ cup brandy
    1 can (14½ oz.) regular-strength beef broth
    1 large onion, finely chopped
    3 large shallots, thinly sliced (about ½ cup)
   ¼ teaspoon white pepper
    3 tablespoons coarse-ground Dijon mustard
    3 medium-size carrots (about 8 oz. *total*), sliced ¼ inch thick
    1 tablespoon margarine
   ¼ pound small mushrooms, quartered
   ¼ cup dry red wine

Cut beef into 1-inch cubes. In a wide 3½- to 4-quart pan, combine beef, brandy, and ¼ cup of the beef broth over medium heat. Cover and simmer for 30 minutes. Add onion, shallots, and pepper; cook, uncovered, stirring occasionally, until most of the liquid has evaporated and juices and onions are browned (about 30 minutes). Add 2 tablespoons of the mustard and remaining 1½ cups beef broth, stirring to loosen any browned bits. Cover, reduce heat, and simmer until beef is almost tender when pierced (1 to 1½ hours). Stir in carrots; cover and continue cooking until carrots are tender (about 30 more minutes).

Meanwhile, melt margarine in an 8- to 9-inch nonstick frying pan over medium-high heat. Add mushrooms and wine; cook, stirring often, until most of the liquid has evaporated and mushrooms are soft. Blend in remaining 1 tablespoon mustard; stir mushroom mixture into stew when carrots are done. Makes 8 servings.

■ *Per serving: 218 calories, 27 g protein, 8 g carbohydrates, 9 g total fat (2 g saturated fat), 67 mg cholesterol, 452 mg sodium*

Czech Beef Stew with Gherkins

Preparation time: About 15 minutes

Cooking time: About 2¼ hours

Paprika and red wine add color and flavor to this hearty Czechoslovakian favorite. Stir the tiny sweet pickles into the stew just before serving.

- 2 **pounds boneless beef bottom round, trimmed of fat**
- ½ **cup water**
- ¼ **teaspoon white pepper**
- 1 **tablespoon salad oil**
- ½ **pound small mushrooms or quartered large mushrooms**
- 1 **large onion, thinly sliced**
- 1 **clove garlic, minced or pressed**
- 1 **tablespoon sweet Hungarian paprika**
- 1 **tablespoon all-purpose flour**
- ½ **cup dry red wine**
- 1 **can (14½ oz.) regular-strength beef broth**
- ½ **cup sweet midget gherkin pickles, drained**
  Salt
- 2 **to 3 cups hot cooked rice**

Cut beef into ¾- by 2-inch strips. In a wide 3½- to 4-quart pan, combine beef, water, pepper, and oil over medium heat. Cover and simmer for 30 minutes. Stir in mushrooms, onion, garlic, and paprika; cook, uncovered, stirring occasionally, until most of the liquid has evaporated and juices and onion are browned (25 to 30 minutes). Add flour, stirring to coat beef and vegetables. Gradually blend in wine and beef broth, stirring to loosen any browned bits.

Cover, reduce heat, and simmer until beef is very tender when pierced (about 1¼ hours). Stir in pickles and season to taste with salt. Serve rice alongside. Makes 6 to 8 servings.

■ *Per serving: 345 calories, 32 g protein, 30 g carbohydrates, 10 g total fat (3 g saturated fat), 77 mg cholesterol, 422 mg sodium*

Baked Brisket of Beef

Preparation time: About 15 minutes

Chilling time: At least 6 hours

Baking time: About 4½ hours

Long, slow, moist cooking tenderizes this coarse-grained cut of meat and brings out its fine flavor. Allowing the seasonings to permeate the meat before cooking helps make it more succulent.

- 2 **tablespoons chili powder**
- 1½ **teaspoons pepper**
- 1 **teaspoon crushed bay leaves**
- ¾ **teaspoon salt or garlic salt**
- 4 **to 5 pounds center-cut fresh beef brisket, trimmed of fat**
- 4 **teaspoons liquid smoke**
  Hot & Spicy Sauce (recipe follows)

Combine chili powder, pepper, bay leaves, and salt. Rub mixture all over meat. Cover and refrigerate for at least 6 hours or until next day.

Place meat in an ungreased 2-inch-deep baking pan. Drizzle liquid smoke over both sides and cover tightly with foil. Bake in a 325° oven until meat is very tender when pierced (about 4½ hours). When meat is almost done, prepare Hot & Spicy Sauce.

Transfer meat to a carving board and cover lightly to keep warm. Skim and discard fat from pan juices; stir juices into sauce. Slice meat thinly across grain at a slant and serve with sauce. Makes 12 to 14 servings.

■ *Per serving: 235 calories, 28 g protein, 1 g carbohydrates, 12 g total fat (4 g saturated fat), 88 mg cholesterol, 230 mg sodium*

Hot & Spicy Sauce. In a 2-quart pan, combine 1 bottle (14 oz. or 1⅓ cups) **catsup**; ½ cup **water**; 1 teaspoon **liquid smoke**; 2 teaspoons **celery seeds**; 3 tablespoons *each* **brown sugar, dry mustard,** and **Worcestershire**; 2 tablespoons **margarine**; and ¼ teaspoon **ground red pepper** (cayenne). Bring to a boil, stirring, over medium-high heat. Makes about 2 cups.

■ *Per tablespoon: 29 calories, .5 g protein, 5 g carbohydrates, 1 g total fat (0 g saturated fat), 0 mg cholesterol, 154 mg sodium*

Barbecued Brisket with Kasha Salad

Preparation time: About 20 minutes

Marinating time: At least 2 hours

Grilling time: 25 to 30 minutes

Cooking time: About 25 minutes

Brisket is excellent when marinated and then grilled just until rare (longer cooking will toughen the meat). Accompany this dish with a buckwheat groat salad studded with grapes.

> 3 **to 3½ pounds center-cut fresh beef brisket, trimmed of fat**
>
> 1 **medium-size onion, finely chopped**
>
> ½ **cup catsup**
>
> 2 **teaspoons prepared horseradish**
>
> ½ **teaspoon whole cloves**
>
> 1 **cinnamon stick (about 2 inches long)**
>
> 2 **tablespoons** *each* **cider vinegar and brown sugar**
>
> ⅓ **cup** *each* **water and dry white wine**
>
> **Unsalted meat tenderizer**
>
> **Kasha Salad (recipe follows)**
>
> **About ½ cup thinly sliced green onions (including tops)**

Place meat in a large plastic bag; add onion, catsup, horseradish, cloves, cinnamon stick, vinegar, brown sugar, water, and wine. Seal bag and rotate to mix well. Refrigerate for at least 2 hours or until next day.

Lift meat from bag and pour marinade into a small pan. Pat meat dry and apply tenderizer, following package directions.

Place meat on a greased grill 4 to 6 inches above a solid bed of low coals. Cook, turning often, until a meat thermometer inserted in thickest part registers 135° to 140° for rare to medium-rare (25 to 30 minutes). Meanwhile, prepare Kasha Salad. Transfer meat to a carving board, cover lightly, and let stand for 10 minutes.

While meat is standing, bring marinade to a boil over medium-high heat. Reduce heat and boil gently, stirring occasionally, for about 5 minutes. Pour through a strainer over salad; garnish salad with green onions. Slice beef thinly across grain at a slant. Makes 8 to 10 servings.

Kasha Salad. Rinse 1½ cups **buckwheat groats** (kasha) and drain well. In a wide nonstick frying pan, stir buckwheat over medium-high heat until grains are dry and smell lightly toasted (2 to 3 minutes).

Stir in 2 cups **regular-strength chicken broth** and 3 tablespoons **lemon juice.** Increase heat to high and bring mixture to a boil; cover, reduce heat, and simmer for 10 minutes. Remove from heat and let stand until liquid has been absorbed (at least 10 minutes).

Transfer to a salad bowl. Measure 4 cups stemmed, rinsed **seedless grapes.** Place a wide nonstick frying pan over high heat. Add 3 cups of the grapes and swirl until fruit is hot and skins begin to pop (1 to 2 minutes). Gently mix hot grapes into kasha; top with remaining grapes.

■ *Per serving: 389 calories, 30 g protein, 42 g carbohydrates, 12 g total fat (4 g saturated fat), 78 mg cholesterol, 445 mg sodium*

■ *Pictured on facing page*

Barbecued Beef & Spinach Patties

Preparation time: About 10 minutes

Grilling time: 8 to 10 minutes

These spinach-flecked beef patties will remind you of a grilled Joe's Special. Eat them with a knife and fork or serve them hamburger-style on sourdough buns with your favorite toppings.

   Tomato–Wine Baste (recipe follows)
1 **egg white**
¼ **cup dry red wine**
⅓ **cup soft bread crumbs**
⅛ **teaspoon pepper**
2 **tablespoons grated Parmesan cheese**
1 **small onion, finely chopped**
1½ **pounds ground lean beef round**
1 **cup finely chopped spinach or ½ cup thawed, well-drained frozen spinach**

Prepare Tomato–Wine Baste and set aside.

In a medium-size bowl, beat together egg white and wine. Stir in bread crumbs, pepper, cheese, and onion; lightly mix in beef and spinach. Shape into 6 patties about ¾ inch thick.

Place patties on a greased grill 4 to 6 inches above a solid bed of medium-hot coals; place pan with basting sauce at edge of grill to warm. Cook patties, turning once and brushing often with sauce, until well browned (8 to 10 minutes *total*). Makes 6 servings.

Tomato–Wine Baste. In a small pan, mix ½ cup canned **tomato sauce**, 2 tablespoons **dry red wine**, 1 tablespoon **Worcestershire**, and 1 large clove **garlic,** minced or pressed.

■ *Per serving: 238 calories, 26 g protein, 5 g carbohydrates, 12 g total fat (5 g saturated fat), 70 mg cholesterol, 263 mg sodium*

Quick Baked Chili

Preparation time: About 10 minutes

Cooking time: About 10 minutes

Baking time: 35 to 45 minutes

Canned black beans bring authentic Mexican flavor to this easy-to-make family dish. If you like, make the chile ahead and refrigerate, then reheat to serve.

   Vegetable oil cooking spray
¾ **pound ground lean beef round**
½ **cup finely chopped celery**
1 **large onion, finely chopped**
1 **clove garlic, minced or pressed**
1 **tablespoon *each* paprika and chili powder**
¼ **teaspoon ground allspice**
1 **large can (15 oz.) tomato sauce**
1 **can (15 oz.) black beans**
¾ **cup water**
½ **cup shredded jack or Cheddar cheese (optional)**

Spray a wide nonstick frying pan with cooking spray. Crumble beef into pan and cook over medium-high heat, stirring often, until beef begins to brown. Stir in celery, onion, garlic, paprika, chili powder, and all-spice. Continue cooking, stirring often, until onion is soft but not browned (3 to 5 minutes). Blend in tomato sauce, beans and their liquid, and water; bring to a boil.

Transfer mixture to a 2- to 2½-quart casserole. Cover and bake in a 350° oven until chili is thick and bubbly (35 to 45 minutes). If desired, sprinkle with cheese just before serving. Makes 4 servings.

■ *Per serving: 331 calories, 26 g protein, 31 g carbohydrates, 12 g total fat (4 g saturated fat), 4 mg cholesterol, 1,130 mg sodium*

*Choose lowfat ground round for tomato and wine-basted
Barbecued Beef & Spinach Patties (recipe on facing page). Bring along
sourdough buns, crisp coleslaw, lemonade, and your favorite
garnishes for a picnic-perfect feast.*

Creamy Meatballs & Artichokes

Preparation time: About 10 minutes

Baking time: About 15 minutes

Cooking time: 8 to 10 minutes

To minimize fat, this dish calls for only the white of an egg to moisten the meatball mixture and yogurt to thicken the sauce. Spoon over white or brown rice.

    1 egg white
    ¾ pound ground lean beef round
    1 medium-size onion, finely chopped
    ¼ cup *each* finely chopped parsley and fine dry bread crumbs
    2 tablespoons pine nuts
    ¾ cup plain lowfat yogurt
    2 tablespoons all-purpose flour
    ½ teaspoon *each* sugar and ground allspice
    1¼ cups regular-strength beef broth
    1 can (14 oz.) artichoke bottoms or artichoke hearts, drained and quartered
       Salt and pepper

In a large bowl, beat egg white slightly. Lightly mix in beef, onion, all but ½ tablespoon of the parsley, and bread crumbs. Shape mixture into 1-inch balls and place slightly apart in a nonstick shallow baking pan. Bake, uncovered, in a 450° oven until well browned (about 15 minutes).

In a wide nonstick frying pan, stir pine nuts over medium-low heat until lightly browned (about 3 minutes); lift out and set aside. Let pan stand until cool. In same pan, blend yogurt, flour, sugar, and allspice; stir in beef broth. Cook over medium heat, stirring constantly, until sauce is bubbling and has thickened. Stir in meatballs, their juices, and artichokes, cooking just until heated through (2 to 3 minutes). Season to taste with salt and pepper. Garnish with pine nuts and remaining parsley. Makes 4 servings.

■ *Per serving: 303 calories, 25 g protein, 18 g carbohydrates, 15 g total fat (5 g saturated fat), 56 mg cholesterol, 420 mg sodium*

Persian Beef & Eggplant Casserole

Preparation time: About 20 minutes

Cooking time: About 20 minutes

Baking time: 45 minutes to 1 hour

This layered eggplant casserole may remind you of moussaka, but it's a lot lighter than the classic version. Allow a few minutes after cooking for food to firm.

    2 medium-size eggplants (about 2 lbs. *total*)
       Olive oil cooking spray
    1½ pounds ground lean beef round
    ½ teaspoon *each* salt, ground nutmeg, and ground cinnamon
    ¼ teaspoon pepper
    3 cloves garlic, minced or pressed
    2 large onions, thinly sliced
    2 tablespoons water
    3 medium-size tomatoes (about 1 lb. *total*), peeled and sliced
       Paprika
    ⅔ to ¾ cup plain lowfat yogurt

Cut eggplants in half lengthwise; then cut crosswise into ½-inch-thick slices. Place in a single layer in greased, shallow, rimmed baking pans; spray with cooking spray. Broil about 4 inches below heat until well browned (6 to 8 minutes); turn slices, spray second sides, and return to broiler until brown. Set aside.

Spray a wide nonstick frying pan with cooking spray. Crumble beef into pan and cook over medium-high heat, stirring often, until browned. Stir in salt, nutmeg, cinnamon, pepper, and garlic. Remove from heat and lift meat mixture from pan; skim and discard fat, if necessary.

Spray pan again with cooking spray. Add onions and water; cook, stirring often, until onions are soft and beginning to brown (about 5 minutes). Set aside.

Line a shallow 3- to 3½-quart casserole with half of the eggplant slices. Cover with beef mixture; then cover with tomato slices. Top with remaining eggplant; then cover evenly with onions and sprinkle generously with paprika. (At this point, you may cover and refrigerate until next day.)

Bake, covered, in a 375° oven until eggplant is very tender when pierced and casserole is bubbling and heated through (45 minutes to 1 hour; about 1¼ hours if cold). Let stand for about 5 minutes before serving. Serve with yogurt. Makes 6 servings.

■ *Per serving: 302 calories, 28 g protein, 19 g carbohydrates, 13 g total fat (5 g saturated fat), 70 mg cholesterol, 266 mg sodium*

Tortilla Chili Pie

Preparation time: About 15 minutes

Cooking time: 6 to 8 minutes

Baking time: About 30 minutes

Overlapping flour tortillas provide the base for this main dish pie. Its hearty filling contains seasoned beef and onions, chili beans, corn, zucchini, and onion.

    Vegetable oil cooking spray
- ½ pound ground lean beef round
- 1 medium-size onion, finely chopped
- 1 teaspoon chili powder
- ½ teaspoon ground cumin
- 1 clove garlic, minced or pressed
- 1 can (8 oz.) tomato sauce
- 1 can (15½ oz.) chili beans
- 1 cup corn (cut from cob or frozen, thawed)
- 1 medium-size zucchini (1 to 6 oz.), diced
- 5 flour tortillas (about 8-inch diameter)
- ½ cup shredded jack or Cheddar cheese

Spray a wide nonstick frying pan with cooking spray. Crumble beef into pan and cook over medium-high heat, stirring often, until lightly browned. Drain off and discard fat. Add onion, chili powder, and cumin; cook, stirring until onion is soft (2 to 3 minutes). Stir in garlic, then add tomato sauce and chili beans. Cook, stirring occasionally, until heated through (about 2 minutes). Remove from heat and stir in corn and zucchini.

Line a 9-inch pie plate with 4 of the flour tortillas, overlapping to fit. Spoon in beef mixture. Cut remaining tortilla into 6 equal triangles and arrange over top. Bake, uncovered, in a 350° oven for 15 minutes; sprinkle with cheese. Continue baking until cheese is golden and filling is bubbly (about 15 more minutes). Makes 4 to 6 servings.

■ *Per serving: 374 calories, 22 g protein, 51 g carbohydrates, 10 g total fat (2 g saturated fat), 38 mg cholesterol, 860 mg sodium*

French Beef & Potato Casserole

Preparation time: About 20 minutes

Cooking time: About 5 minutes

Baking time: About 1½ hours

Layer seasoned ground beef and potatoes in a large casserole, pour a beef bouillon mixture over all, and bake until potatoes are lightly browned and tender.

    Olive oil cooking spray
- 1 pound ground lean beef round
- 1 large tomato, peeled and diced
- ½ teaspoon salt
- ¼ teaspoon pepper
- 6 cloves garlic, minced or pressed
- 2 teaspoons dry thyme leaves
- 1 teaspoon dry marjoram leaves
- 4 pounds white, thin-skinned potatoes
- 2 or 3 bay leaves (optional)
- 1 beef bouillon cube dissolved in 1 cup hot water

Spray a wide nonstick frying pan with cooking spray; also spray a 4-quart casserole and set aside.

Crumble beef into pan and cook over medium-high heat, stirring often, until meat loses its pink color.

Stir in tomato, salt, pepper, garlic, thyme, and marjoram. Remove from heat and set aside.

Peel potatoes and slice about ¼ inch thick. Place about a fifth of the potatoes in a layer in the bottom of sprayed casserole; top with a fourth of the meat mixture. Repeat layers of potatoes and meat mixture, ending with potatoes. Lay bay leaves, if used, on top; spray lightly with cooking spray. Slowly pour bouillon mixture over all. Cover and bake in a 375° oven until potatoes are lightly browned on top and very tender when pierced (about 1½ hours). Let stand, covered, for about 10 minutes before serving. Makes 6 servings.

■ *Per serving: 388 calories, 21 g protein, 51 g carbohydrates, 11 g total fat (4 g saturated fat), 48 mg cholesterol, 376 mg sodium*

*Elegant for Sunday dinner or any other festive occasion, Franca's
Roast Lamb (recipe on page 53) includes pan-roasted new potatoes and
a luscious gravy made with the wine and rosemary bath in
which the leg of lamb marinated.*

Lamb

Leg
Loin
Rib
Shoulder

Most cuts of lamb are low in calories because they're low in fat. Located largely on the outside of pieces and in layers between muscles, lamb fat is relatively easy to trim, especially from the larger cuts. How well the fat is trimmed before cooking and how the lamb is prepared influence the amount of fat in a cooked serving. The illustration on page 52 identifies the lean cuts.

Leg. The meat from a leg of lamb is juicy, full-flavored, and tender. It can be cooked by dry-heat methods (roasting, broiling, grilling), either with or without a marinade. Cooked by moist heat methods—whether in the oven or in a range-top stew—the meat from a leg of lamb will be tender in far less time than most cuts of beef.

A full-cut leg, which includes the sirloin, may weigh as much as 10 pounds. Many butchers now sell the sirloin portion separately; what's left is called a three-quarter (or short-cut) leg. Sometimes, the leg is sold divided into three portions: sirloin, shank, and center roast.

Loin. Tender, juicy lamb loin adjoins the leg, and sirloin steaks can be cut from this large end of the leg. Dry-heat cooking methods (roasting, broiling, grilling) work well. The loin is usually divided into chops, but it's also sold as a boneless double loin roast or a bone-in loin roast.

Rib. Cuts from the rib lie next to the loin, toward the front of the lamb. They are adaptable to all types of dry-heat cooking (roasting, broiling, grilling). Rib chops, with most of the meat in a single morsel next to the bone, are the most familiar form. When not cut apart, rib chops make a small bone-in roast. And in its fanciest form, the rib can be prepared as a dramatic (although not very meaty) crown roast.

Shoulder. Lamb shoulder is comprised of several small muscles separated by layers of fat and connective tissue. Chops from the shoulder can be cooked by dry-heat methods (pan-broiling, broiling, grilling), but they will be most tender if cooked no more than to the medium-rare stage. Shoulder chops can also be prepared using moist heat (braised or otherwise cooked gently with a little liquid). The most available forms are blade and arm chops; Saratoga chops are rolled and skewered boneless blade chops.

Pictured on page 50

Franca's Roast Lamb

Preparation time: About 15 minutes

Marinating time: At least 4 hours

Roasting time: About 2 hours

An Italian living in Australia devised this dish for a restaurant in Mudgee, a Gold Rush town northwest of Sydney now noted for its wines. Small halved red potatoes tucked beneath the roasting lamb absorb its savory juices.

- 1 leg of lamb (5½ to 6 lbs.)
- 4 cloves garlic
- 2 cups dry white wine such as Australian or California dry Semillon
- 3 tablespoons fresh rosemary or 1 table- spoon dry rosemary
- 1 tablespoon olive oil
- 16 to 20 small red thin-skinned potatoes, *each* 1½ to 2 inches in diameter
- 2 teaspoons *each* margarine and all- purpose flour
  Salt and pepper
  Rosemary sprigs (optional)

Trim and discard surface fat from lamb. Thinly slice 2 cloves of the garlic; make small, shallow cuts in surface of lamb and insert a garlic slice in each.

In a large plastic bag set in a pan, combine wine, rosemary, oil, and remaining 2 cloves of garlic (minced or pressed). Add lamb, turning to coat. Seal bag and refrigerate for at least 4 hours or until next day; turn bag over once or twice.

Scrub potatoes and cut in half; place in a roasting pan, cut sides down. Place rack in pan. Remove lamb from marinade, reserving marinade. Place lamb on rack and insert a meat thermometer in thickest part. Roast, uncovered, in a 350° oven until thermometer registers 135° to 140° for medium-rare (about 2 hours). Transfer lamb and potatoes to a platter and keep warm. Skim and discard fat from pan, if necessary.

Place pan over medium heat and add margarine; let stand until melted. Blend in flour. Gradually stir in reserved marinade. Cook, stirring, until sauce is boiling and has thickened; season to taste with salt and pepper. Thinly slice lamb. Serve with potatoes and pass sauce at the table. Garnish with rosemary sprigs, if desired. Makes 8 to 10 servings.

■ *Per serving: 397 calories, 43 g protein, 22 g carbohydrates, 14 g total fat (4 g saturated fat), 129 mg cholesterol, 120 mg sodium*

Curry & Honey-glazed Lamb Mini-Roast

Preparation time: About 10 minutes

Roasting time: 25 to 40 minutes

Boneless leg of lamb is rolled and tied into a compact roast, then basted with a piquant-sweet glaze of curry and honey. The meat cooks quickly, so check the meat thermometer often.

- 1 to 1½ pounds boneless leg of lamb
- 2 tablespoons honey
- 1 teaspoon salad oil
- 1½ teaspoons lemon juice
- ½ teaspoon curry powder
- ⅛ teaspoon coarsely ground pepper

Trim and discard surface fat from lamb. Roll lamb compactly; then tie securely with string at 1½-inch intervals. Combine honey, oil, lemon juice, curry powder, and pepper and set aside.

Place lamb on a rack in a roasting pan; spoon honey mixture over lamb, turning to coat. Insert a meat thermometer in center. Roast, uncovered, in a 425° oven until thermometer registers 135° to 140° for rare to medium-rare (25 to 40 minutes); after 20 minutes, check temperature every 5 minutes. Let lamb stand, lightly covered, for about 5 minutes, then slice thinly across the grain. Makes 4 to 6 servings.

■ *Per serving: 198 calories, 24 g protein, 7 g carbohydrates, 8 g total fat (2 g saturated fat), 76 mg cholesterol, 59 mg sodium*

Cider-baked Lamb Stew with Turnips

Preparation time: About 25 minutes

Baking time: 1¾ to 2½ hours

In this easy version of a French country favorite, floured lamb cubes are browned in the oven at high heat without additional fat, then simmered in cider with vegetables until tender. Baked sweet potatoes and steamed fresh spinach complement the stew.

   3   tablespoons all-purpose flour
   ¼   teaspoon white pepper
   ½   teaspoon ground cloves
   2   pounds boneless leg of lamb, trimmed
       of fat
   1½ cups apple cider
   4   medium-size turnips (about 1¼ lbs.
       total), peeled and cut lengthwise
       into wedges
   2   medium-size onions, sliced
   1   clove garlic, minced or pressed
   ⅓   cup chopped parsley
       Salt

Combine flour, pepper, and cloves. Cut lamb into 1-inch cubes; coat with flour mixture, shaking off excess. Arrange cubes slightly apart in an ungreased 9- by 13-inch baking dish or pan. Bake, uncovered, in a 500° oven for 20 minutes. Remove dish from oven and let stand for about 5 minutes to cool slightly.

Meanwhile, reduce oven temperature to 375°. Gradually add cider to lamb, stirring to loosen any browned bits. Add turnips, onions, garlic, and all but 1 tablespoon of the parsley.

Cover tightly with lid or foil and bake, stirring once or twice, until lamb and turnips are very tender when pierced (1½ to 2 hours). Season to taste with salt. Garnish with remaining parsley. Makes 8 servings.

■ *Per serving: 202 calories, 24 g protein, 13 g carbohydrates, 5 g total fat (2 g saturated fat), 73 mg cholesterol, 112 mg sodium*

■ *Pictured on facing page*

Apricot & Cinnamon-spiced Lamb

Preparation time: About 15 minutes

Baking time: 1½ to 2 hours

Moroccan in inspiration, this stew features apricots plumped in the lamb's honey-sweetened juices.

   2   pounds boneless leg of lamb, trimmed
       of fat
   ¼   cup honey
   1   large onion, chopped
   2   cloves garlic, minced or pressed
   1   cinnamon stick (about 3 inches long)
   2   tablespoons lemon juice
   1½ teaspoons turmeric
   ½   teaspoon salt
   1   cup moist-pack dried apricots
   ¼   to ½ cup water (optional)
       Lemon slice
       Cilantro (coriander) sprigs

Cut lamb into 1-inch cubes. In a 3- to 3½-quart casserole, combine lamb, honey, onion, garlic, cinnamon, lemon juice, turmeric, and salt; cover tightly. Bake in a 350° oven, stirring once or twice, until lamb is very tender when pierced (1½ to 2 hours). About 15 minutes before lamb is done, stir in dried apricots.

Remove from oven; if mixture seems dry, stir in water as needed. Garnish with lemon slice and cilantro. Makes 8 servings.

■ *Per serving: 227 calories, 24 g protein, 21 g carbohydrates, 5 g total fat (2 g saturated fat), 73 mg cholesterol, 211 mg sodium*

Cooked in its own juices until tender, succulent Apricot & Cinnamon-spiced Lamb (recipe on facing page) crowns fluffy steamed couscous. Honey and spices add intriguing flavors to meat and fruit in this North African entrée.

Shashlik

Preparation time: About 35 minutes

Marinating time: At least 2 hours

Grilling time: 8 to 10 minutes

Lamb cubes are first seasoned with a wine marinade, then threaded onto metal skewers with small whole onions and squares of red bell pepper.

- 2 **pounds boneless leg of lamb, trimmed of fat**
- 1 **small onion, finely chopped**
- 1 **tablespoon *each* salad oil and Worcestershire**
- 1 **bay leaf**
- 1 **clove garlic, minced or pressed**
- ¼ **teaspoon pepper**
- 2 **tablespoons chopped parsley**
- 1 **teaspoon dry oregano leaves**
- 1 **cup dry red wine**
- 1 **pound small onions, *each* about 1 inch in diameter**
- 2 **medium-size red bell peppers (about 12 oz. *total*), seeded and cut into 1-inch squares**
  Salt and pepper

Cut lamb into 1-inch cubes; place in a heavy plastic bag set in a bowl. To bag, add chopped onion, oil, Worcestershire, bay leaf, garlic, pepper, parsley, oregano, and wine. Seal bag and turn over to mix ingredients. Refrigerate for at least 2 hours or until next day, turning bag once or twice.

Meanwhile, in a 3-quart pan, combine small whole onions with enough water to cover. Bring to a boil; then reduce heat and boil gently for 5 minutes. Drain and peel onions. (At this point, you may cover and refrigerate until next day.)

Remove lamb from bag, reserving marinade. Thread onto 8 metal skewers, each about 14 inches long, alternating lamb with small whole onions and red pepper squares.

Place skewers on a lightly greased grill 4 to 6 inches above a solid bed of hot coals. Cook, brushing with marinade and turning as needed, until lamb is evenly browned but still pink in center; cut to test (8 to 10 minutes *total*). Season to taste with salt and pepper. Makes 8 servings.

■ *Per serving: 199 calories, 25 g protein, 7 g carbohydrates, 7 g total fat (2 g saturated fat), 76 mg cholesterol, 70 mg sodium*

Plum-glazed Grilled Loin Chops

Preparation time: About 10 minutes

Cooking time: About 20 minutes

Grilling time: About 10 minutes

A fresh plum glaze, edged with red onion, mustard, and lemon juice, adds a sophisticated touch to grilled lamb chops.

- 2 **teaspoons salad oil**
- 1 **small red onion, finely chopped**
- 12 **ounces red plums, pitted and chopped (about 2 cups *total*)**
- 2 **teaspoons *each* dry mustard and soy sauce**
- 2 **tablespoons sugar**
- 1 **tablespoon lemon juice**
- 8 **loin lamb chops, *each* about 1 inch thick (about 2½ lbs. *total*), trimmed of fat**
  Salt

Heat oil in a 1½- to 2-quart pan over medium heat. Add onion and plums; cook, stirring occasionally, until onion is soft (about 5 minutes). Add mustard, soy sauce, sugar, and lemon juice, stirring until sugar is dissolved. Bring to a gentle boil; then continue cooking, stirring often, until mixture has thickened (about 15 minutes). (At this point, you may let cool, cover, and refrigerate for up to 3 days; return to room temperature before continuing.)

Place lamb on a lightly greased grill 4 to 6 inches above a solid bed of medium-hot coals. Cook, brushing generously with plum mixture and turning once, until lamb is well browned but still pink in center; cut to test (about 10 minutes *total*). Season to taste with salt. Offer remaining plum sauce to spoon over individual portions. Makes 8 servings.

■ *Per serving: 206 calories, 25 g protein, 4 g carbohydrates, 9 g total fat (3 g saturated fat), 80 mg cholesterol, 114 mg sodium*

■ *Per tablespoon plum sauce: 25 calories, 0 g protein, 4 g carbohydrates, 1 g total fat (0 g saturated fat), 0 mg cholesterol, 43 mg sodium*

Minted Loin Lamb Chops

Preparation time: About 5 minutes

Broiling time: 8 to 10 minutes

A tangy mint sauce flavors these broiled chops. Drizzle extra sauce over tiny red potatoes or steamed baby carrots.

3 tablespoons mint jelly

2 tablespoons white wine vinegar

1 tablespoon soy sauce

2 tablespoons minced fresh mint leaves or 2 teaspoons dry mint leaves

2 teaspoons Dijon mustard

¼ teaspoon pepper

1 clove garlic, minced or pressed

4 loin lamb chops, *each* about 1 inch thick (about 1¼ lbs. *total*), trimmed of fat

Mint sprigs

Salt

In a small pan, melt jelly over low heat, stirring occasionally. Remove from heat and stir in vinegar, soy sauce, minced mint, mustard, pepper, and garlic.

Place lamb on a rack in a broiler pan. Brush generously with some of the jelly mixture. Broil about 4 inches below heat until well browned on both sides, turning once and brushing second sides with more of the jelly mixture (8 to 10 minutes *total* for medium-rare). Garnish with mint sprigs and season to taste with salt. Serve with remaining jelly mixture to add to taste. Makes 4 servings.

■ *Per serving: 228 calories, 25 g protein, 11 g carbohydrates, 8 g total fat (3 g saturated fat), 80 mg cholesterol, 405 mg sodium*

Spicy Lamb Skewers with Baked Lemon Pilaf

Preparation time: About 20 minutes

Marinating time: At least 3 hours

Baking time: 45 to 50 minutes

Grilling time: 8 to 10 minutes

The fruit- and curry-flavored marinade for this lamb dish originated in South Africa. The pilaf cooks in the oven while the skewered meat grills.

1 large onion, finely chopped

1 teaspoon salad oil

3 tablespoons cider vinegar

1 tablespoon curry powder

1 bay leaf

2 teaspoons chili powder

½ teaspoon salt

1 clove garlic, minced or pressed

¾ cup apricot nectar

2 pounds boneless lamb loin, trimmed of fat

Baked Lemon Pilaf (recipe follows)

In a medium-size pan, combine onion, oil, and vinegar over medium-low heat. Cook, stirring, until most of the vinegar has evaporated and onion is soft (about 5 minutes). Stir in curry powder, bay leaf, chili powder, salt, garlic, and apricot nectar; reduce heat to low and simmer for 5 minutes. Cut lamb into 1-inch cubes.

Place lamb in a bowl and mix with apricot marinade. Cover and refrigerate for at least 3 hours or up to 8 hours. About 1 hour before cooking lamb, prepare Baked Lemon Pilaf.

Lift lamb from marinade, reserving marinade. Discard bay leaf. Thread lamb onto 8 skewers. Place on a greased grill 4 to 6 inches above a solid bed of hot coals. Cook, brushing with remaining marinade and turning as needed, until lamb is well browned but still pink in center; cut to test (8 to 10 minutes *total*). Serve with pilaf. Makes 8 servings.

Baked Lemon Pilaf. Spray a deep 2-quart baking dish with **vegetable oil cooking spray.** Stir in 3 cups **regular-strength chicken broth,** 1½ cups **long-grain white rice,** 1 tablespoon **grated lemon peel,** 3 tablespoons **lemon juice,** ⅓ cup thinly sliced **green onions** (including tops), and 2 teaspoons **margarine.** Cover tightly and bake in a 350° oven until rice is tender (45 to 50 minutes). Fluff with a fork.

■ *Per serving: 348 calories, 28 g protein, 34 g carbohydrates, 10 g total fat (3 g saturated fat), 77 mg cholesterol, 542 mg sodium*

*Treat family or guests to assertive Lean Lamb Curry (recipe on facing
page), served with steamed rice and a varied selection of condiments. For
flavor contrasts to the savory meat mixture, top with cool yogurt and cucumber, spicy chutney, salty peanuts, and sweet raisins and bananas.*

■ Pictured on facing page

Lean Lamb Curry

Preparation time: About 25 minutes

Cooking time: About 30 minutes

In this appealing entrée, strips of lamb are browned quickly, then cooked with vegetables, apple, and seasonings. Serve over rice with a selection of condiments, which add contrasting textural and flavor accents.

1   pound boneless lamb loin, trimmed of fat

1   tablespoon salad oil

1   large onion, thinly sliced

1   tablespoon curry powder

½   teaspoon *each* ground ginger and ground cumin

2   cloves garlic, minced or pressed

1   medium-size carrot (about 3 oz.), thinly sliced

1   small tart apple, peeled, cored, and chopped

1   small green bell pepper, seeded and cut into thin bite-size strips

1   can (14½ oz.) regular-strength beef broth

    Salt and cayenne

2   to 3 cups hot cooked rice

    Condiments (optional; suggestions follow)

Cut lamb across the grain into bite-size strips about ¼ inch thick; set aside.

Heat oil in a wide nonstick frying pan over medium-high heat. Add about half the lamb, cooking and turning just until browned on all sides; lift out. Repeat with remaining lamb. To the same pan, add onion, curry powder, ginger, and cumin. Reduce heat to medium-low and cook, stirring often, until onion is soft (about 3 minutes). Stir in garlic, carrot, apple, green pepper, and beef broth. Increase heat to medium-high and boil gently, stirring occasionally, until carrots are tender when pierced and sauce has thickened slightly (about 20 minutes). Stir in lamb just until heated through. Season to taste with salt and cayenne. Serve with rice and, if desired, condiments. Makes 4 servings.

Condiments. Choose from the following, arranged in separate bowls: sliced **banana; chutney; plain low-fat yogurt;** chopped **dry-roasted peanuts;** chopped **cucumber; raisins.**

■ *Per serving: 417 calories, 29 g protein, 47 g carbohydrates, 12 g total fat (3 g saturated fat), 75 mg cholesterol, 465 mg sodium*

Rib Chops Juniper

Preparation time: About 10 minutes

Cooking time: 12 to 15 minutes

This elegant, slimmed-down version of a French bistro classic features lamb chops rubbed with fragrant juniper berries and topped with a wine-shallot sauce.

    Juniper Berry Paste (recipe follows)

8   single-rib lamb chops (about 1¼ lbs. *total*), trimmed of fat

    Vegetable oil cooking spray

½   cup *each* dry red wine and regular-strength beef broth

2   tablespoons finely chopped shallots

1   tablespoon margarine

    Watercress sprigs

Prepare Juniper Berry Paste; rub evenly over both sides of each chop.

Coat a wide frying pan with cooking spray and place over medium-high heat. Add lamb and cook, turning once, until well browned on both sides but still pink in center; cut to test (about 8 minutes *total*). Remove lamb to a platter and keep warm.

To same pan, add wine, beef broth, and shallots; increase heat to high and bring mixture to a boil, stirring to loosen any browned bits. Boil until reduced to about ⅓ cup (about 3 minutes). Remove from heat and melt in margarine. Pour wine mixture over lamb; garnish with watercress. Makes 4 servings.

Juniper Berry Paste. Coarsely crush 1½ tablespoons **dry juniper berries.** Mix with ½ teaspoon **coarsely ground pepper** and 1 large clove **garlic,** minced or pressed.

■ *Per serving: 237 calories, 24 g protein, 2 g carbohydrates, 14 g total fat (4 g saturated fat), 78 mg cholesterol, 224 mg sodium*

Feature

Grinding Lamb for Mediterranean & North African Entrées

Standard ground lamb contains too much fat to qualify as lean meat. Ask your butcher to grind lamb loin or other well-trimmed lean cuts for you. Or grind it yourself using a food processor or food chopper (with the fine disc in place).

To grind lamb using the processor, have the meat at refrigerator temperature. (If meat has been frozen, thaw it in the refrigerator until very few ice crystals remain.) Trim and discard any connective fibers, gristle, and fat. Cut lamb into 1-inch chunks. Place up to ¾ pound at a time in the work bowl with the metal knife. Chop, using on-off pulses, until the lamb is as fine as you like it. Now you're ready to cook any of these lively Mediterranean and North African dishes.

In a 2-quart pan, bring beef broth to a boil over high heat; stir in rice. Reduce heat to low, cover, and simmer until rice is tender and broth has been absorbed (20 to 25 minutes).

Meanwhile, stir pine nuts in a wide nonstick frying pan over medium-low heat until lightly browned (about 3 minutes); remove from pan and set aside. Spray the same pan with cooking spray and place over medium-high heat. Crumble in lamb and cook, stirring, just until browned. Stir in onion, garlic, cinnamon, water, and raisins. Cover, reduce heat to low, and simmer for 5 minutes.

Shortly before rice is done, stir spinach into lamb mixture. Cook, uncovered, stirring often, just until spinach is wilted and turns bright green (2 to 3 minutes). Season to taste with salt and pepper. Spoon rice into a warm deep platter; top with lamb mixture and garnish with pine nuts. Makes 4 to 6 servings.

■ *Per serving: 360 calories, 26 g protein, 46 g carbohydrates, 8 g total fat (2 g saturated fat), 60 mg cholesterol, 435 mg sodium*

Ground Lamb & Spinach Pilaf

- 2 cups regular-strength beef broth
- 1 cup long-grain white rice
- 2 tablespoons pine nuts
  Olive oil cooking spray
- 1 pound ground lean lamb loin
- 1 large onion, finely chopped
- 1 clove garlic, minced or pressed
- ½ teaspoon ground cinnamon
- ⅓ cup water
- ½ cup raisins
- 1 bunch (about 12 oz.) spinach, rinsed, stemmed, and cut into 1-inch-wide strips
  Salt and pepper

Moroccan Lamb Patties

- 1 egg white
- ⅓ cup evaporated skim milk
- ¼ cup *each* soft bread crumbs and chopped parsley
- ½ teaspoon *each* salt and ground cumin
- ¼ teaspoon *each* ground coriander and ground red pepper (cayenne)
- 1 small onion, finely chopped
- 1 pound ground lean lamb loin
- ¼ to ⅓ cup plain lowfat yogurt
  Chopped fresh mint

In a medium-size bowl, combine egg white and milk; beat until blended. Stir in bread crumbs, parsley, salt, cumin, coriander, red pepper, and onion. Add lamb and mix just until combined. Shape mixture into 4 patties, each about ¾ inch thick.

Place patties on lightly greased rack of a broiler pan. Broil about 3 inches below heat, turning once, until golden brown on both sides but still pink in center; cut to test (8 to 10 minutes *total*). To serve, spoon a dollop of yogurt over each patty and garnish with mint. Makes 4 servings.

■ *Per serving: 229 calories, 29 g protein, 6 g carbohydrates, 9 g total fat (3 g saturated fat), 83 mg cholesterol, 410 mg sodium*

Sesame Lamb Meatballs

- ½ cup plain lowfat yogurt
- 3 tablespoons chopped fresh mint leaves or 1½ tablespoons dry mint leaves
- 1 pound ground lean lamb loin
- ½ cup finely chopped parsley
- 5 tablespoons wheat germ
- 2 tablespoons water
- 1 clove garlic, minced or pressed
- ½ teaspoon *each* salt and dry rosemary
- ¼ teaspoon *each* pepper and ground allspice
- 1 egg white
- ¼ cup sesame seeds

Stir together yogurt and 2 tablespoons of the fresh mint (or 1 tablespoon of the dry mint). Cover and refrigerate. In a medium-size bowl, combine lamb, parsley, 2 tablespoons of the wheat germ, water, garlic, salt, rosemary, pepper, allspice, and remaining mint. Mix lightly; then shape into 1¼-inch meatballs.

In a shallow pan, beat egg white slightly; in another shallow pan, mix sesame seeds and remaining 3 tablespoons of the wheat germ. Dip meatballs in egg white; then coat well with sesame seed mixture. Arrange meatballs slightly apart on lightly greased rack of a broiler pan.

Bake, uncovered, in a 425° oven until firm and golden brown (about 20 minutes). Offer with yogurt mixture to spoon over meatballs to taste. Makes 4 to 6 servings.

■ *Per serving: 228 calories, 24 g protein, 8 g carbohydrates, 11 g total fat (3 g saturated fat), 61 mg cholesterol, 294 mg sodium*

Lamb Meatball & Lentil Soup

Olive oil cooking spray
- 1 large onion, finely chopped
- 2 cups plus 2 tablespoons water
- 2 cloves garlic, minced or pressed
- 1 teaspoon *each* dry thyme leaves and ground cumin
- ¼ teaspoon whole allspice
- 1 bay leaf
- 1 cinnamon stick (about 3 inches long)
- 1 cup finely chopped celery
- 2 medium-size carrots (about 6 oz. *total*), thinly sliced
- 1½ cups lentils, rinsed and drained
- 1 can (15 oz.) tomato purée
- 6 cups regular-strength low-sodium chicken broth

Lamb Meatballs (recipe follows)
- 4 cups coarsely shredded fresh spinach leaves

Salt and pepper

Coat a 5- to 6-quart pan with cooking spray. Add onion and 2 tablespoons of the water. Cook, stirring often, over medium heat until onion is soft but not browned (about 5 minutes). Stir in garlic, thyme, cumin, allspice, bay leaf, cinnamon stick, celery, and carrots. Add lentils, tomato purée, chicken broth, and remaining 2 cups water. Bring to a boil; reduce heat to medium-low, cover, and boil gently until lentils and vegetables are very tender (about 1 hour).

Meanwhile, prepare Lamb Meatballs. Add meatballs to soup. Cover, increase heat to medium, and cook until meatballs are cooked through; cut to test (about 20 minutes). Stir in spinach and continue cooking, uncovered, just until leaves are wilted and bright green (2 to 3 minutes). Discard bay leaf and cinnamon stick. Season to taste with salt and pepper. Makes 6 servings.

Lamb Meatballs. In a medium-size bowl, beat 1 **egg white** slightly. Mix in ¼ cup finely chopped **onion**, ¾ pound **ground lean lamb loin**, ¼ teaspoon *each* **pepper** and **ground cinnamon**, ½ teaspoon **salt,** and 3 tablespoons chopped fresh **parsley.** Shape into 1-inch balls.

■ *Per serving: 347 calories, 31 g protein, 45 g carbohydrates, 6 g total fat (2 g saturated fat), 37 mg cholesterol, 630 mg sodium*

Luau Lamb Chops with Sesame Rice

Preparation time: About 20 minutes

Cooking time: About 25 minutes

Grilling time: About 8 minutes

Grilled chops take a Polynesian twist when basted with a ginger-flavored glaze. Serve with pineapple slices and fluffy rice with toasted sesame seeds.

- 1 **small pineapple (2 to 2½ lbs.)**
- ¼ **cup firmly packed brown sugar**
- 1 **teaspoon** *each* **dry mustard, ground ginger, and soy sauce**
  Sesame Rice (recipe follows)
- 8 **single-rib lamb chops (about 1½ lbs.** *total***), trimmed of fat**

Peel and core pineapple; cut crosswise into ½-inch-thick slices. Place 2 of the slices in a blender or food processor, reserving the rest; whirl until puréed. Press through a strainer into a measuring cup; you should have about ⅓ cup juice. In a small pan, combine pineapple juice, brown sugar, mustard, ginger, and soy sauce. Bring to a boil over medium-high heat, stirring until sugar has dissolved; set aside.

Prepare Sesame Rice. About 10 minutes before rice is done, place lamb chops and reserved pineapple slices on a lightly greased grill 4 to 6 inches above a solid bed of medium-hot coals (place pineapple at cooler edges of grill). Cook, brushing well with pineapple juice mixture and turning once, until pineapple is golden brown and lamb is well browned but still pink in center; cut to test (about 8 minutes *total*). Serve lamb chops and grilled pineapple with rice. Makes 4 servings.

Sesame Rice. Toast 2 tablespoons **sesame seeds** in a 2- to 3-quart pan over medium heat until golden (3 to 5 minutes), shaking pan often. Remove from pan and set aside. In same pan, combine 1½ cups **regular-strength chicken broth,** 1 teaspoon **soy sauce,** and ½ teaspoon **salad oil;** bring to a boil over high heat. Add ¾ cup **long-grain white rice.** Reduce heat to low, cover, and simmer until rice is tender (about 20 minutes). Fluff with a fork; sprinkle with sesame seeds and about 2 tablespoons thinly sliced **green onions** (including tops).

■ *Per serving: 484 calories, 30 g protein, 60 g carbohydrates, 15 g total fat (4 g saturated fat), 81 mg cholesterol, 641 mg sodium*

■ *Pictured on facing page*

Grilled Rib Chops, Abruzzi Style

Preparation time: About 15 minutes

Cooking time: 10 to 12 minutes

Grilling time: About 8 minutes

This recipe reflects its origins in Italy's mountainous Abruzzi region, where sheep graze on the high plateaus, and herbs, greens, and beans are locally grown.

- 2 **teaspoons olive oil**
- 1 **teaspoon Italian herb seasoning or ¼ teaspoon** *each* **dry basil, oregano, thyme, and marjoram leaves**
- 3 **cloves garlic, minced or pressed**
- ½ **teaspoon crushed dried hot red chiles**
- 8 **single-rib lamb chops (about 1¼ lbs.** *total***), trimmed of fat**
- 1 **bunch (about 12 oz.) red Swiss chard, rinsed and stemmed**
- 1 **small onion, finely chopped**
- 1 **can (15 oz.) white kidney beans (cannellini), drained**
- 1 **tablespoon red wine vinegar**
  Salt and pepper

In a small bowl, combine 1 teaspoon of the oil, herb seasoning, garlic, and chiles. Rub about two-thirds of the mixture over tops of lamb chops; set aside.

Coarsely chop chard and place in a wide frying pan with about ½ inch of water. Bring to a boil over high heat; reduce heat to medium and cook, uncovered, for 3 minutes. Drain well and set aside.

Place lamb, seasoned sides down, on a lightly greased grill 4 to 6 inches above a solid bed of medium-hot coals. Cook, turning once, until well browned but still pink in center; cut to test (about 8 minutes *total*).

Meanwhile, heat remaining 1 teaspoon oil in a wide nonstick frying pan over medium heat; add onion and remaining garlic mixture. Cook, stirring often, until soft but not brown (about 5 minutes); add chard and beans. Cook, stirring gently, until heated through (about 2 minutes). Stir in vinegar. Season to taste with salt and pepper. Serve lamb chops with chard mixture. Makes 4 servings.

■ *Per serving: 322 calories, 29 g protein, 19 g carbohydrates, 14 g total fat (4 g saturated fat), 81 mg cholesterol, 485 mg sodium*

*Juicy lamb from the barbecue tops herbed red chard and white
beans in Grilled Rib Chops, Abruzzi Style (recipe on facing page). This
satisfying Italian dish is quick to prepare and cook.*

Oven Lamb Stew with Apples

Preparation time: About 30 minutes

Baking time: 2½ to 3 hours

Cubed lamb shoulder needs no browning before it goes into a deep casserole to make an oven stew. Tart apples, white wine, and tangy malt vinegar balance the lamb's naturally sweet flavor.

2 to 2½ **pounds boneless lamb shoulder, trimmed of fat**

¾ **teaspoon dry rosemary**

¼ **teaspoon pepper**

2 **cloves garlic, minced or pressed**

2 **medium-size tart apples, cored, peeled, and sliced ¼ inch thick**

5 **medium-size carrots (about 1 lb. *total*), thinly sliced**

1 **can (14½ oz.) pear-shaped tomatoes**

½ **cup dry white wine**

2 **tablespoons malt vinegar**

1 **tablespoon Worcestershire**

1 **tablespoon all-purpose flour blended with 2 tablespoons water**

Salt

Cut lamb into 1-inch cubes, then mix with rosemary, pepper, and garlic. Place about a third of the lamb in a deep 3- to 3½-quart casserole and cover with apple slices. Add another third of the lamb and cover with carrots; then add remaining lamb.

In a food processor or blender, whirl tomatoes and their liquid until puréed. Mix in wine, vinegar, and Worcestershire; pour over lamb. Bake, tightly covered, in a 375° oven until lamb is very tender when pierced; stir once or twice after the first hour of baking (2½ to 3 hours *total*). Skim and discard surface fat, if necessary. Stir flour mixture into stew. Continue baking, covered, until liquid bubbles (about 5 more minutes). Season to taste with salt. Makes 8 servings.

■ *Per serving: 245 calories, 26 g protein, 14 g carbohydrates, 9 g total fat (3 g saturated fat), 84 mg cholesterol, 215 mg sodium*

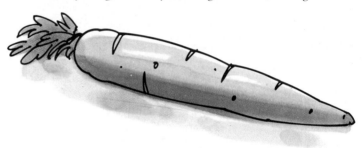

Malaysian Lamb with Spiced Onions

Preparation time: About 20 minutes

Cooking time: 1½ to 1¾ hours

This crimson stew proclaims its Southeast Asian roots with the flavors of green chile, garlic, turmeric, and ginger.

2 **pounds boneless lamb shoulder, trimmed of fat**

½ **cup water**

2 **large onions, sliced ¼ inch thick**

1 **tablespoon cider vinegar**

1 **teaspoon chili powder**

1 **can (4 oz.) diced green chiles**

1 **tablespoon grated fresh ginger**

1 **clove garlic, minced or pressed**

½ **teaspoon *each* salt and ground turmeric**

1 **can (1 lb.) tomatoes**

1 **tablespoon chopped cilantro (coriander)**

3 **cups hot cooked rice**

Cilantro sprigs

Cut lamb into 1-inch cubes; then combine with water, onions, vinegar, and chili powder in a wide 3½- to 4-quart pan over medium-low heat. Cover and simmer for 30 minutes. Increase heat to medium and cook, uncovered, stirring occasionally, until most of the liquid has evaporated (30 to 35 minutes). Stir in green chiles, ginger, garlic, salt, and turmeric; then add tomatoes (break up with a spoon) and their liquid, stirring to loosen any browned bits from pan.

Cover, reduce heat to low, and simmer until lamb is very tender when pierced (30 to 40 more minutes). Stir in chopped cilantro. Skim and discard fat, if necessary. Spoon over rice and garnish with cilantro sprigs. Makes 6 to 8 servings.

■ *Per serving: 336 calories, 29 g protein, 32 g carbohydrates, 9 g total fat (3 g saturated fat), 86 mg cholesterol, 458 mg sodium*

Simmered Shoulder Chops & Red Pepper

Preparation time: About 15 minutes

Cooking time: About 1 hour

In this colorful Basque-style dish, lamb chops simmer in a ruddy tomato and bell pepper sauce. Add a generous amount of parsley just before serving.

> Olive oil cooking spray
> 4 small lamb shoulder blade chops (1½ to 2 lbs. *total*), trimmed of fat
> 2 teaspoons olive oil
> 1 large onion, finely chopped
> 1 large red bell pepper (about 8 oz.), seeded and cut into thin strips
> 2 large cloves garlic, minced or pressed
> 1 can (8 oz.) tomato sauce
> ½ cup regular-strength chicken broth
> ¼ cup chopped parsley
> Salt and pepper

Spray a wide nonstick frying pan with cooking spray and place over medium-high heat. Add lamb and brown well on both sides; then remove from pan and set aside.

Drain and discard fat from pan, if necessary. Heat oil in same pan over medium heat; add onion and red pepper. Cook, stirring often, until onion is soft but not brown (3 to 5 minutes). Stir in garlic, tomato sauce, and chicken broth. Bring to a boil; then return lamb to pan. Reduce heat, cover, and simmer until lamb is very tender when pierced (40 to 45 minutes).

Lift lamb from sauce to a serving dish and keep warm. Increase heat to high and stir in most of the parsley; bring to a boil, cooking until sauce has thickened (about 3 minutes). Season to taste with salt and pepper; then spoon over lamb. Garnish with remaining parsley. Makes 4 servings.

■ *Per serving: 299 calories, 31 g protein, 10 g carbohydrates, 15 g total fat (4 g saturated fat), 101 mg cholesterol, 576 mg sodium*

Breton Lamb Chops with White Beans

Preparation time: About 10 minutes

Cooking time: 1¾ to 2 hours

Standing time: 1 hour

Lamb chops, browned just before serving, top white beans in this French country-style dish; you can cook and refrigerate the beans up to two days ahead.

> Cooked White Beans (recipe follows)
> 2 teaspoons margarine
> 2 medium-size onions, finely chopped
> ⅛ teaspoon ground allspice
> ¾ teaspoon dry thyme leaves
> ⅔ cup regular-strength chicken broth
> 2 cloves garlic, minced or pressed
> 2 teaspoons all-purpose flour
> ⅓ cup dry white wine
> Salt and pepper
> Vegetable oil cooking spray
> 4 small lamb shoulder blade chops (1½ to 2 lbs. *total*), trimmed of fat
> Chopped parsley

Prepare Cooked White Beans.

In a wide frying pan, melt margarine over medium heat. Add onions, allspice, thyme, and 2 tablespoons of the chicken broth; cook, stirring often, until onions are soft but not brown (8 to 10 minutes). Stir in garlic, then sprinkle with flour. Gradually blend in wine and remaining broth. Mix in beans; reduce heat to low, cover, and simmer for 30 minutes. Season to taste with salt and pepper.

Shortly before beans are done, spray a wide nonstick frying pan with cooking spray and place over medium-high heat. Add lamb and cook, turning once, until well browned on both sides but still slightly pink in center; cut to test (about 8 minutes *total*). Spoon beans into a deep platter; top with lamb and garnish with parsley. Makes 4 servings.

Cooked White Beans. Sort 1½ cups **dried small white beans** to remove any debris. Rinse and drain. In a 4-quart pan, bring 6 cups **water** to a boil over high heat. Add beans and boil for 2 minutes. Remove from heat, cover, and let stand for 1 hour. Drain and rinse beans; then set aside.

In same pan, bring 4½ cups **water** to a boil with ½ teaspoon **salt**. Add beans, reduce heat to medium-high, and boil gently, partially covered, until tender when pierced (45 minutes to 1 hour); drain well.

■ *Per serving: 544 calories, 47 g protein, 55 g carbohydrates, 15 g total fat (5 g saturated fat), 101 mg cholesterol, 579 mg sodium*

Vibrant Caribbean flavors—cumin, garlic, lime, chiles, and bell pepper—permeate Cuban-style Mini-Roast with Black Beans & Rice (recipe on page 69); spoon the savory beans over the rice. To heighten the tropical taste, garnish with lime wedges and sautéed banana quarters coated in cinnamon sugar.

Pork

Leg

Tenderloin

Loin

Finding lowfat cuts of pork is less of a challenge than in years past. The little piggy that comes to market today is much leaner than it's ever been before. And cuts from the loin and leg are the leanest of all.

As for preparation, we've long been told that pork must be cooked until it's well done. But we now know that the parasites sometimes found in pork are destroyed at an internal temperature of 137° F. So pork cooked to 150° to 155°— at which point it's still moist, tender, and slightly rosy—is well within the bounds of safety. By all means use a reliable meat thermometer when cooking pork, especially for the thicker cuts.

Leg. Most pork legs are cured and sold as ham, but more fresh boneless legs are being offered today than in the past. Butchers often cut and package this cut as boneless slices, strips, or cubes. Bone-in fresh ham (as it's sometimes labeled) is easiest to find during the holiday season, when it can be counted on to provide an ample, impressive centerpiece for a Christmas or New Year's Day dinner table.

Boned, pork leg yields enough meat for more than one family meal. You might roll and tie an under-two-pound portion to make a quick-cooking small roast; cut the remainder into bite-size pieces for stew, a stir-fry, or to grill on skewers.

In any case, pork from the leg is moist and quite tender. You can cook it by dry-heat methods (roasting, broiling, and grilling) or by simmering it in liquid (such as wine or broth).

Tenderloin. Pork tenderloin is a boneless strip of meat that lies inside the rib cage of the loin. As the name suggests, it's an exceedingly tender cut. Often, two of these choice cuts are packaged together for a total of one and a quarter to just under two pounds of meat. Tenderloin is an ideal choice for dry-heat cooking in the oven, on the barbecue, or—with a minimum of added fat—sautéing in a nonstick skillet.

Loin. All the pork that comes from the loin section is tender and can be cooked using either dry heat (roasting, broiling, grilling, sautéing) or moist heat (braising, stewing). Center-cut chops from the loin contain some of the tenderloin; rib chops don't. Both boneless and bone-in loin roasts are good choices for either oven roasting or cooking on a covered barbecue by indirect heat.

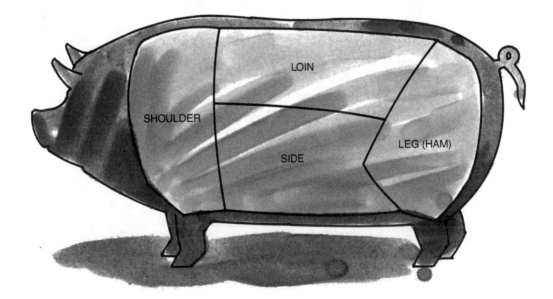

■ *Pictured on page 66*

Cuban-style Mini-Roast with Black Beans & Rice

Preparation time: About 15 minutes

Marinating time: At least 4 hours

Cooking time: About 8 minutes

Baking time: 35 to 55 minutes

A compact roast of succulent leg of pork—sometimes called fresh ham—is marinated Caribbean style and served with rice and savory black beans.

- 1½ to 1¾ pounds boneless fresh leg of pork, trimmed of fat
- 2 cloves garlic, minced or pressed
- ½ teaspoon dry oregano leaves
- ¼ teaspoon cumin seeds, coarsely crushed
- ¼ teaspoon crushed dried hot red chiles
- ¼ cup lime juice
  Cuban Black Beans (recipe follows)
- 3 cups hot cooked long-grain white rice
- ¼ cup thinly sliced green onions (including tops)
  Lime wedges
  Cilantro (coriander) sprigs

Roll pork compactly; then tie securely with string at 1½-inch intervals. In a large plastic bag set in a pan, combine garlic, oregano, cumin seeds, chiles, and lime juice; add pork, turning to coat. Seal bag and refrigerate for at least 4 hours or until next day, turning bag over once or twice.

Remove pork from bag, reserving marinade. Place on a rack in a roasting pan and insert a meat thermometer in center. Roast, uncovered, in a 350° oven, drizzling once or twice with marinade, until thermometer registers 155° for pork that's slightly pink in center (35 to 55 minutes); after 25 minutes, check temperature every 5 to 10 minutes. Meanwhile, prepare Cuban Black Beans.

Lift pork onto a platter and let stand, lightly covered, for about 5 minutes; then slice thinly across the grain. Garnish pork and rice with green onions, lime, and cilantro; serve with beans. Makes 6 servings.

Cuban Black Beans. Heat 2 teaspoons **olive oil** in a wide nonstick frying pan over medium heat. Add 1 medium-size **onion** (thinly sliced) and ½ cup finely chopped **green bell pepper;** cook, stirring often, until onion is soft but not brown (about 5 minutes). Stir in 1 clove **garlic** (minced or pressed), ½ teaspoon **ground cumin,** and 1 can (15 oz.) **black beans** and their liquid. Cook until heated through (about 3 minutes). Just before serving, stir in 2 teaspoons **cider vinegar.**

■ *Per serving: 427 calories, 34 g protein, 43 g carbohydrates, 12 g total fat (4 g saturated fat), 87 mg cholesterol, 336 mg sodium*

Pork & Sauerkraut Stew

Preparation time: About 15 minutes

Cooking time: About 1¾ hours

Egg noodles and rye bread are good foils for this tangy stew, seasoned with garlic, dill, and paprika.

- 1½ pounds boneless fresh leg of pork, trimmed of fat
- ¼ teaspoon salt
- ⅛ teaspoon white pepper
- 1 tablespoon salad oil
- 1 large onion, finely chopped
- 1 can (14½ oz.) regular-strength chicken broth
- 2 cloves garlic, minced or pressed
- 2 teaspoons paprika
- 1 large jar (22 oz.) or can (27 oz.) sauerkraut, drained
- 1½ teaspoons dry dill weed
- ½ cup plain lowfat yogurt blended with 2 teaspoons cornstarch
  Chopped parsley

Cut pork into 1-inch cubes. In a wide 3½- to 4-quart pan, combine pork, salt, pepper, oil, onion, and ½ cup of the chicken broth over medium-low heat. Cover and simmer for 30 minutes. Stir in garlic and paprika. Increase heat to medium and cook, uncovered, stirring occasionally, until most of the liquid has evaporated (about 30 minutes). Meanwhile, rinse sauerkraut, drain, and set aside.

Add remaining broth to pan, stirring to loosen any browned bits. Mix in dill and sauerkraut. Cover, reduce heat to low, and simmer until pork is very tender when pierced (35 to 40 more minutes).

Skim and discard surface fat, if necessary. Add yogurt mixture; increase heat to medium-high and cook, stirring constantly, until mixture has thickened and is bubbling. Garnish with parsley. Makes 6 servings.

■ *Per serving: 221 calories, 26 g protein, 7 g carbohydrates, 9 g total fat (3 g saturated fat), 78 mg cholesterol, 699 mg sodium*

Pork with Red Peppers & Clams

Preparation time: About 20 minutes

Marinating time: 6 to 8 hours

Cooking time: 1¾ to 2 hours

Pork from the land and clams from the sea mingle in a traditional Portuguese main dish that goes well with a crisp green salad and crusty bread.

Wine Marinade (recipe follows)
- 1½ **pounds boneless fresh leg of pork, trimmed of fat**
- 2 **teaspoons olive oil**
- 2 **medium-size onions, thinly sliced**
- 2 **medium-size tomatoes, peeled and chopped**
- ⅛ **teaspoon crushed dried hot red chiles**
- 2 **medium-size red bell peppers (about 12 oz. *total*), seeded and cut into thin strips**
- 12 **to 18 small hard-shell clams, suitable for steaming, scrubbed**
- ¼ **cup chopped cilantro (coriander)**

Prepare Wine Marinade. Cut pork into 1-inch cubes and add to marinade. Seal bag and refrigerate for 6 to 8 hours. Lift out pork, reserving marinade.

In a wide 3½- to 4-quart pan, combine pork, ½ cup of the marinade, oil, and onions over medium-low heat. Cover and simmer for 30 minutes. Increase heat to medium and cook, uncovered, stirring occasionally, until most of the liquid has evaporated (30 to 35 minutes). Add tomatoes, dried chiles, and remaining marinade, stirring to loosen any browned bits from pan.

Cover, reduce heat to low, and simmer until pork is tender when pierced (30 to 40 more minutes). Add bell peppers and clams. Cover and simmer until clams pop open (15 to 20 minutes); then stir in cilantro. Ladle into wide bowls. Makes 6 servings.

Wine Marinade. In a large plastic bag set in a pan, combine 1½ cups **dry white wine**, 2 **bay leaves**, ½ teaspoon **salt**, 1 teaspoon **paprika**, and 3 cloves **garlic** (minced or pressed).

■ *Per serving: 226 calories, 29 g protein, 8 g carbohydrates, 8 g total fat (2 g saturated fat), 90 mg cholesterol, 151 mg sodium*

Pork Picadillo

Preparation time: About 15 minutes

Cooking time: About 1½ hours

Though *picadillo* literally means hash, this cinnamon- and currant-laced stew of tender pork is quite festive. Spoon it into warm corn tortillas and roll up into soft tacos to eat as finger food.

- 1½ **pounds boneless fresh leg of pork, trimmed of fat**
- 1 **tablespoon salad oil**
- 1 **medium-size onion, finely chopped**
- ½ **cup water**
- 1 **clove garlic, minced or pressed**
- 1 **can (8 oz.) tomato sauce**
- ¼ **cup tomato-based chili sauce**
- ½ **teaspoon *each* salt, ground cinnamon, and ground cumin**
- ¼ **cup dried currants**
- 2 **tablespoons cider vinegar**
- 1 **tablespoon brown sugar**
- 4 **green onions, thinly sliced (including tops)**
- 1 **lime, cut in wedges**

Cut pork into ¾-inch cubes. In a wide 3½- to 4-quart pan, combine pork, oil, onion, and water over medium-low heat. Cover and simmer for 30 minutes. Increase heat to medium and cook, uncovered, stirring occasionally, until most of the liquid has evaporated (25 to 30 minutes). Add garlic, tomato sauce, chili sauce, salt, cinnamon, cumin, currants, vinegar, and sugar, stirring to loosen any browned bits from pan.

Cover, reduce heat to low, and simmer until pork is very tender when pierced with a fork (30 to 35 more minutes). Garnish with green onions and offer with lime. Makes 6 servings.

■ *Per serving: 236 calories, 25 g protein, 16 g carbohydrates, 9 g total fat (2 g saturated fat), 77 mg cholesterol, 628 mg sodium*

Iberian cooks are clever at linking meat and shellfish in a single hearty dish. In Spain, the result is paella. One Portuguese combination is Pork with Red Peppers & Clams (recipe on facing page). Serve it with dry white wine, a warm baguette, and your favorite flan or crème caramel.

Pan-browned Ham with Braised Fennel

Preparation time: About 10 minutes

Cooking time: About 10 minutes

Anise-flavored fennel accents a quick-cooking ham slice. Look for feathery bunches of this distinctive vegetable in the fall and early winter.

1 pound fennel

2 teaspoons olive oil or salad oil

1 slice (about 1 lb.) center-cut cooked ham, trimmed of fat

⅓ cup dry white wine or regular-strength chicken broth

¼ teaspoon pepper

Rinse fennel thoroughly; trim and discard base and any discolored or bruised portions. Trim and discard coarse tops of stalks, reserving green leaves. Cut bulb lengthwise into quarters; slice thinly. Chop enough leaves to make 2 to 3 tablespoons; reserve remaining leaves.

Heat oil in a wide frying pan over medium-high heat. Add ham and brown on both sides, turning once (about 5 minutes *total*). Lift onto a platter and keep warm. To pan, add sliced fennel, wine, and pepper. Cook, stirring often, until fennel is tender and only 2 tablespoons of the liquid remain (about 5 minutes). Stir in chopped fennel leaves; then spoon mixture around ham. Garnish with reserved fennel leaves. Cut ham into serving pieces. Makes 4 servings.

■ *Per serving: 187 calories, 23 g protein, 4 g carbohydrates, 8 g total fat (2 g saturated fat), 53 mg cholesterol, 1,725 mg sodium*

Pounded Pork Tenderloin with Orange-Pepper Sauce

Preparation time: About 15 minutes

Cooking time: About 10 minutes

Sliced and pounded thin, pork tenderloin captures the zest of fresh orange and coarsely crushed black pepper in a wine-shallot sauce.

12 ounces pork tenderloin, trimmed of fat and silvery membrane

About 3 tablespoons all-purpose flour

2 tablespoons margarine

¼ cup chopped shallots

¾ teaspoon black peppercorns, coarsely crushed

⅓ cup dry white wine

1 tablespoon finely shredded orange peel

⅔ cup orange juice

Cut pork across the grain into ½-inch slices; then place between pieces of plastic wrap. Using the flat side of a meat mallet, pound gently and evenly until meat is ¼ inch thick. Remove plastic wrap and dust pork lightly with flour.

In a wide nonstick frying pan, melt 1 tablespoon of the margarine over medium-high heat. Add about half of the pork (don't crowd slices) and cook, turning once, until golden brown on both sides (about 1 minute *total*). Lift onto a platter, cover lightly, and keep warm in a 200° oven. Melt remaining tablespoon margarine in pan and cook remaining pork as above; then add to platter in oven.

To pan, add shallots and pepper. Cook, stirring, until shallots are soft (about 2 minutes). Add wine, orange peel, and orange juice. Increase heat to high and bring to a boil, stirring often; cook until reduced to ½ cup (4 to 5 minutes). Pour sauce over pork. Makes 3 servings.

■ *Per serving: 262 calories, 25 g protein, 15 g carbohydrates, 11 g total fat (2 g saturated fat), 74 mg cholesterol, 149 mg sodium*

Roast Tenderloin Oriental

Preparation time: About 15 minutes

Roasting time: 35 to 40 minutes

Cooking time: 3 to 5 minutes

Supermarkets often sell lean pork tenderloins in packages of two; tie the two together to make a quick-cooking, single small roast. Hoisin and oyster sauces, sherry, garlic, and fresh ginger flavor this version. Serve with rice and a steamed green vegetable.

Oriental Baste (recipe follows)

2 **pork tenderloins (about 1½ lbs.** *total***), trimmed of fat and silvery membrane**

1 **medium-size onion, finely chopped**

⅓ **cup** *each* **regular-strength beef broth and dry sherry**

Prepare Oriental Baste; set aside. Place one tenderloin atop the other, the narrow end of one aligned with the wide end of the other. Tie together securely with string at 1½-inch intervals to make a single roast. Place in a greased shallow roasting pan and brush generously with basting mixture. Insert a meat thermometer in thickest part. Pat onion around meat.

Roast, uncovered, in a 425° oven, drizzling two or three times with most of the remaining baste, until thermometer registers 155° for pork that's slightly pink in center (35 to 40 minutes). Lift pork onto a platter and keep warm. To drippings and onion in pan, add any remaining basting mixture, beef broth, and sherry. Place over medium-high heat, stirring to loosen any browned bits. Boil until reduced to about ¾ cup. Slice pork across the grain and serve with sauce. Makes 6 servings.

Oriental Baste. Mix ¼ cup **hoisin sauce;** 2 tablespoons *each* **oyster sauce, dry sherry,** and grated **fresh ginger;** and 2 cloves **garlic** (minced or pressed).

■ *Per serving: 166 calories, 25 g protein, 8 g carbohydrates, 3 g total fat (1 g saturated fat), 74 mg cholesterol, 681 mg sodium*

Peppered Pork Tenderloin with Green Onion Sauce

Preparation time: About 10 minutes

Roasting time: 35 to 40 minutes

Cooking time: About 5 minutes

Here's another quick entrée in which two tenderloins are bound together so the meat will cook equally throughout. Pat crushed multicolored peppercorns over the pork roast before cooking.

2 **pork tenderloins (about 1½ lbs.** *total***), trimmed of fat and silvery membrane**

1 **tablespoon coarsely crushed multicolored or black peppercorns**

⅔ **cup dry white wine**

1 **tablespoon margarine**

2 **teaspoons** *each* **soy sauce and Dijon mustard**

1 **teaspoon honey**

½ **cup diagonally sliced green onions (including tops)**

Place one tenderloin atop the other, the narrow end of one aligned with the wide end of the other. Tie together securely with string at 1½-inch intervals to make a single roast. Place on a rack in a greased shallow roasting pan; firmly pat pepper all over pork.

In a small pan, combine wine, margarine, soy sauce, mustard, and honey over medium heat; stir until mixture simmers. Remove from heat and drizzle a little of the mixture over pork. Insert a meat thermometer in thickest part. Roast, uncovered, in a 425° oven, basting once with wine mixture, until thermometer registers 155° for pork that's slightly pink in center (35 to 40 minutes *total*). Lift pork onto a platter and keep warm.

Pour remaining wine mixture into roasting pan; place over medium-high heat and stir to loosen any browned bits. Bring to a boil; stir in green onions and remove from heat. Slice pork across the grain and serve with sauce. Makes 6 servings.

■ *Per serving: 156 calories, 24 g protein, 3 g carbohydrates, 5 g total fat (1 g saturated fat), 74 mg cholesterol, 244 mg sodium*

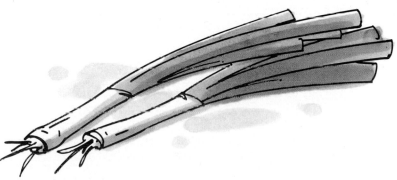

Fruits coax a beguiling sweetness from pork, as in these richly glazed Black Currant Pork Chops (recipe on facing page). Black currant preserves and raspberry vinegar deserve credit for the enticing flavors that emerge.

Roast Pork Loin with Apple Chutney

Preparation time: About 25 minutes

Marinating time: At least 2 hours

Roasting time: 1 to 1¼ hours

Cooking time: 20 to 25 minutes

A tangy fresh fruit chutney and a crusty coating of savory seasonings and honey transform a simple roast into an elegant autumn dinner entrée.

> Apple Chutney (recipe follows)
>
> 1 tablespoon honey
>
> 1 tablespoon minced fresh sage leaves or 1 teaspoon dry sage leaves
>
> 1 clove garlic, minced or pressed
>
> 1 teaspoon crushed juniper berries
>
> ¼ teaspoon coarsely ground pepper
>
> 1 boned, rolled, and tied center-cut pork loin roast (2 to 2¼ lbs.), trimmed of fat
>
> ½ cup *each* apple cider and regular-strength beef broth

Prepare Apple Chutney; set aside. In a small bowl, combine honey, sage, garlic, juniper berries, and pepper. Place pork in a shallow baking dish and spoon on honey mixture to coat. Cover and refrigerate for at least 2 hours or until next day, turning occasionally.

Place pork on a rack in a shallow roasting pan and insert a meat thermometer in thickest part. Roast, uncovered, in a 350° oven until thermometer registers 155° for pork that's slightly pink in center (1 to 1¼ hours). Lift pork onto a platter and keep warm.

Spoon off and discard fat in pan, if needed. Place pan over medium-high heat; add cider and beef broth, stirring to loosen any browned bits. Boil, stirring occasionally, until reduced to about ½ cup (3 to 5 minutes). Slice roast thinly across the grain; then drizzle with sauce. Serve with chutney. Makes 8 servings.

■ *Per serving: 210 calories, 27 g protein, 4 g carbohydrates, 9 g total fat (3 g saturated fat), 76 mg cholesterol, 132 mg sodium*

Apple Chutney. Peel, core, and chop 2 large tart **green apples** (about 1 lb. *total*); seed and finely chop ½ **lemon** (including peel). Combine apples; lemon; ⅓ cup finely chopped **onion**; ½ cup seeded, finely chopped **red bell pepper**; 2 tablespoons grated **fresh ginger**; and 1 clove **garlic** (minced or pressed).

In a 2- to 3-quart pan, combine ⅓ cup **cider vinegar** and ⅔ cup firmly packed **brown sugar** over high heat, stirring until sugar has dissolved. Add apple mixture, ⅛ teaspoon **ground red pepper** (cayenne), and ½ teaspoon **salt**. Bring to a boil, reduce heat to medium-low, and boil gently, uncovered, stirring often, until chutney has thickened and is reduced to about 2 cups (about 20 minutes). If made ahead, let cool, cover, and refrigerate for up to a week. Serve at room temperature. Makes about 2 cups.

■ *Per tablespoon: 52 calories, 0 g protein, 14 g carbohydrates, 0 g total fat (0 g saturated fat), 0 mg cholesterol, 72 mg sodium*

■ *Pictured on facing page*

Black Currant Pork Chops

Preparation time: About 5 minutes

Cooking time: 16 to 20 minutes

These succulent chops are glazed with fruit preserves accented by mustard and tart vinegar. Serve them on a bed of golden egg noodles.

> 6 center-cut loin pork chops (about 2 lbs. *total*), trimmed of fat
>
> Freshly ground pepper
>
> Vegetable oil cooking spray
>
> 3 tablespoons black currant preserves or currant jelly
>
> 1½ tablespoons Dijon mustard
>
> ¼ cup raspberry vinegar or white wine vinegar
>
> Watercress sprigs
>
> Raspberries and huckleberries (optional)

Sprinkle pork chops generously with pepper. Spray a wide frying pan with cooking spray and place over medium-high heat. Add chops and brown well on both sides, turning once (8 to 10 minutes *total*). While chops are browning, mix preserves and mustard; spoon over chops. Reduce heat to medium-low. Cover and cook until chops are still moist and look slightly pink in center; cut to test (6 to 8 more minutes). Lift chops onto a platter and keep warm.

Add vinegar to mixture in pan. Increase heat to medium-high, stirring to loosen any browned bits. Boil sauce, uncovered, until reduced to about ¼ cup (2 to 3 minutes). Spoon sauce over chops. Garnish with watercress and, if desired, berries. Makes 6 servings.

■ *Per serving: 228 calories, 27 g protein, 8 g carbohydrates, 9 g total fat (3 g saturated fat), 76 mg cholesterol, 194 mg sodium*

Feature

Lean but Juicy
Barbecued Pork

The mouth-watering succulence of barbecued pork—accented with fresh herbs, sweet spices, piquant chiles, marinades, even pesto—is hard to resist. By starting with well-trimmed cuts such as loin chops, tenderloin, or leg, you can enjoy distinctive smoke-tinged dishes that satisfy your tastebuds without the extra fat of more traditional barbecue fare.

Thai-seasoned Loin Chops with Cilantro Pesto

    1   teaspoon grated lemon peel
    4   cloves garlic
    ¼   cup *each* chopped fresh ginger and shallots
    1   tablespoon chili powder
    ½   teaspoon *each* ground coriander, pepper, and crushed dried hot red chiles
    1   teaspoon anchovy paste
    3   tablespoons water
        Cilantro Pesto (recipe follows)
    6   boneless center-cut loin pork chops (about 1½ lbs. *total*), trimmed of fat
        Hot sweet mustard (optional)

In a blender or food processor, combine lemon peel, garlic, ginger, shallots, chili powder, coriander, pepper, crushed chiles, anchovy paste, and water. Whirl, stopping motor to scrape down sides of container once or twice, until a smooth paste forms; set aside. (At this point, you may cover and refrigerate until next day.) Prepare Cilantro Pesto.

Generously coat both sides of pork chops with chile paste. Place chops, well apart, between sheets of plastic wrap. Using flat side of a meat mallet, pound evenly until each piece is about ¼ inch thick.

Place on a greased grill 4 to 6 inches above a solid bed of hot coals. Cook, turning once, until lightly browned but still moist and faintly pink in center; cut to test (5 to 7 minutes *total*). Serve with Cilantro Pesto and, if desired, mustard. Makes 6 servings.

■ *Per serving: 223 calories, 25 g protein, 3 g carbohydrates, 12 g total fat (4 g saturated fat), 78 mg cholesterol, 110 mg sodium*

Cilantro Pesto. In a blender or food processor, combine 3 cups lightly packed **cilantro** (coriander), 1 clove **garlic,** and 3 tablespoons **olive oil;** whirl until puréed. Season to taste with **salt.** Makes about ½ cup.

■ *Per tablespoon: 47 calories, 0 g protein, 0 g carbohydrates, 5 g total fat (1 g saturated fat), 0 mg cholesterol, 2 mg sodium*

Grilled Pork Tenderloin in Raspberry-Herb Marinade

        Raspberry-Herb Marinade (recipe follows)
    2   pork tenderloins (about 1½ lbs. *total*), trimmed of fat and silvery membrane
    2   tablespoons olive oil
    8   to 10 cups bite-size pieces mixed salad greens (such as red- or green-leaf lettuce, radicchio, watercress, and arugula), rinsed and crisped
        Salt

Prepare Raspberry-Herb Marinade. Pour 6 tablespoons of the marinade into a heavy plastic bag set in a shallow pan. Add tenderloins and seal bag, turning to coat with marinade. Refrigerate for at least 2 hours or until next day, turning bag once or twice. Meanwhile, light coals in a covered barbecue; when coals are covered with gray ash, push to either side of grate. Stir oil into remaining marinade; cover and set aside.

Lift tenderloins from marinade and drain. Place in center of a lightly greased grill 4 to 6 inches above the coals. Cover and cook, basting several times, until a meat thermometer inserted in center of thickest part registers 155° (20 to 30 minutes).

When pork is nearly done, lightly mix reserved marinade and salad greens in a large bowl. Place pork on a platter and slice across the grain. Season greens and pork to taste with salt and serve together. Makes 6 servings.

Raspberry-Herb Marinade. Combine ½ cup **raspberry vinegar;** 2 cloves **garlic** (minced or pressed); 1 tablespoon *each* **honey** and **Dijon mustard;** 1 teaspoon *each* **fresh marjoram, sage,** and **thyme leaves** (or ¼ teaspoon *each* of the dry herbs); and ½ teaspoon coarsely ground **pepper.** Mix until well blended.

■ *Per serving: 211 calories, 27 g protein, 5 g carbohydrates, 9 g total fat (2 g saturated fat), 84 mg cholesterol, 122 mg sodium*

Barbecued Pork Tenderloin

1	clove garlic, minced or pressed
¾	teaspoon ground ginger
⅛	teaspoon crushed dried hot red chiles
½	teaspoon dry mustard
2	tablespoons brown sugar
½	teaspoon grated orange peel
1	tablespoon *each* salad oil and soy sauce
3	tablespoons rice vinegar
1	pork tenderloin (about 12 oz.), trimmed of fat and silvery membrane
1	teaspoon cornstarch

In a shallow bowl, stir together garlic, ginger, chiles, mustard, brown sugar, orange peel, oil, soy sauce, and vinegar. Add tenderloin, turning to coat. Cover and refrigerate for at least 30 minutes or up to 3 hours, turning several times. Lift tenderloin from bowl, reserving marinade. Place on a lightly greased grill 4 to 6 inches above a solid bed of medium-hot coals. Cook, brushing with marinade and turning two or three times to brown all sides, until a meat thermometer inserted into thickest part regis-

ters 155° (about 20 minutes *total*). Lift onto a platter and keep warm.

Add water to remaining marinade to make ½ cup liquid. Blend in cornstarch. Pour into a small pan and bring to a boil over high heat, stirring constantly, until thickened. Slice pork across the grain and serve with sauce. Makes 3 servings.

■ *Per serving: 215 calories, 24 g protein, 11 g carbohydrates, 7 g total fat (2 g saturated fat), 74 mg cholesterol, 404 mg sodium*

Pork Satay Balinese

2	pounds boneless fresh leg of pork or pork loin, trimmed of fat
½	cup Major Grey's chutney
¼	cup catsup
1	tablespoon *each* salad oil and soy sauce
4	drops liquid hot pepper seasoning
¼	cup very finely chopped dry-roast peanuts
	Cilantro (coriander) sprigs

Cut pork into 1-inch cubes. In a blender or food processor, combine chutney, catsup, oil, soy sauce, and hot pepper seasoning; whirl until smooth. Place pork cubes in a heavy plastic bag set in a shallow pan. Add chutney mixture and seal bag, turning to coat. Refrigerate for at least 2 hours or until next day.

Lift pork from bag, reserving marinade; thread onto 8 skewers. Arrange on a lightly greased grill 4 to 6 inches above a solid bed of medium-hot coals. Cook, basting once or twice with marinade, turning as needed, until well browned on all sides (12 to 15 minutes *total*). Arrange on a serving dish, sprinkle with peanuts, and garnish with cilantro. Makes 8 servings.

■ *Per serving: 246 calories, 25 g protein, 14 g carbohydrates, 10 g total fat (3 g saturated fat), 77 mg cholesterol, 315 mg sodium*

Hickory Baked Pork Chops

Preparation time: About 10 minutes

Baking time: About 1 hour

Cooking time: 3 to 4 minutes

The smoky taste of hickory seasons these tender pork chops, which bake in the oven in a flavorful tomato-based sauce. Serve over fresh fettuccine with the sauce.

    1 **small can (8 oz.) stewed tomatoes**

    1 **small onion, thinly sliced**

    1 **clove garlic, minced or pressed**

    1 **teaspoon *each* sugar and dry oregano**

    1 **can (8 oz.) tomato sauce**

    2 **tablespoons hickory smoke–flavored barbecue sauce**

    4 **center-cut loin pork chops (about 1¼ lbs. *total*), trimmed of fat**

    1 **package (9 oz.) fresh fettuccine**
       Chopped parsley

In a shallow 2-quart casserole, stir together stewed tomatoes (break up with a spoon) and their liquid, onion, garlic, sugar, oregano, tomato sauce, and barbecue sauce. Add pork chops, spooning about half of the tomato mixture over them. Cover and bake in a 350° oven until pork near bone is slightly pink; cut to test (about 1 hour).

When chops are almost done, cook fettuccine in a 5- to 6-quart pan in 3 quarts boiling water just until tender (3 to 4 minutes); or cook according to package directions. Drain well.

Transfer fettuccine to a warm deep platter. Lift chops from sauce and arrange over pasta; spoon on a little of the sauce and garnish with parsley. Serve with remaining sauce to add to taste. Makes 4 servings.

■ *Per serving: 413 calories, 35 g protein, 46 g carbohydrates, 10 g total fat (3 g saturated fat), 146 mg cholesterol, 643 mg sodium*

■ *Pictured on facing page*

Pork Stir-fry with Litchis

Preparation time: About 15 minutes

Marinating time: At least 1 hour

Cooking time: About 8 minutes

Canned litchis lend their exotic perfume to this stir-fry of marinated pork strips and thinly sliced green onions. Serve with steamed rice.

    1 **can (1 lb. 4 oz.) litchis or longans, packed in syrup**

  ¼ **cup soy sauce**

    2 **tablespoons very finely chopped fresh ginger**

    1 **clove garlic, minced or pressed**

    1 **pound boneless pork loin, trimmed of fat**

    2 **teaspoons salad oil**

    4 **green onions (including tops), thinly sliced**

    2 **cups hot cooked long-grain white rice**
       Green onion brushes (optional)

Drain litchis, reserving ½ cup of the syrup; cover fruit and refrigerate. In a plastic bag set in a pan, combine soy sauce, ginger, garlic, and reserved syrup.

Cut pork across the grain into bite-size strips about ¼ inch thick and 2 to 3 inches long. Add to soy sauce mixture, seal bag, and refrigerate for at least 1 hour or until next day.

Lift pork from bag, reserving marinade. Heat 1 teaspoon of the oil in a wide nonstick frying pan over high heat. Add half of the pork and cook, turning as needed, until browned on all sides; then remove from pan. Repeat with remaining oil and pork (about 6 minutes *total*). To pan add marinade, pork and its juices, litchis, and sliced green onions. Stir gently until boiling. Serve with rice and garnish with green onion brushes, if desired. Makes 4 servings.

■ *Per serving: 447 calories, 28 g protein, 59 g carbohydrates, 11 g total fat (3 g saturated fat), 68 mg cholesterol, 1,153 mg sodium*

There's little oil or other fat in Pork Stir-fry with Litchis (recipe on facing page). Before cooking, marinate strips of boneless pork loin in sweet litchi syrup enhanced with soy sauce, ginger, and garlic. Steamed bok choy and aromatic Chinese tea complete the menu.

Spicy Stir-fried Pork & Vegetables

Preparation time: About 20 minutes

Cooking time: About 12 minutes

Colorful vegetables mingle with lean pork in this chile-spiked family dish. Serve with a basket of warm corn tortillas.

- 1 **pound boneless pork loin, trimmed of fat**
- 2 **tablespoons dry white wine or lemon juice**
- 1½ **teaspoons dry oregano leaves**
- ¾ **teaspoon ground cumin**
- 1 **clove garlic, minced or pressed**
- 1 **medium-size onion**
- 4 **teaspoons olive oil**
- 1 **pound zucchini, sliced ¼ inch thick**
- 1 **small red bell pepper (about 4 oz.), seeded and finely chopped**
- 1 **cup corn (cut from cob or frozen, thawed)**
- 1 **can (4 oz.) diced green chiles**
- 3 **tablespoons water**
- 1 **medium-size tomato, peeled and cut into thin wedges**
  Salt and pepper

Cut pork into bite-size slices about ¼ inch thick. In a bowl, combine pork, wine, oregano, cumin, and garlic; set aside. Cut onion in half crosswise, then lengthwise; cut quarters into ½-inch-thick wedges. Heat 1 teaspoon of the oil in a wide nonstick frying pan over high heat. Add onion and cook, stirring, for 1 minute. Add zucchini, bell pepper, corn, chiles, and water. Cook, stirring, just until zucchini is tender-crisp (about 5 minutes). Lift from pan and place in a bowl; set aside.

Heat 1½ teaspoons of the remaining oil in same pan. Add half the pork mixture and cook, turning as needed, until lightly browned (about 2 minutes); remove from pan and add to vegetable mixture. Repeat with remaining 1½ teaspoons oil and pork mixture. Return all the pork, any remaining marinade, and vegetables to pan, stirring just until hot (about 1 minute). Gently stir in tomato; season to taste with salt and pepper. Makes 4 to 6 servings.

■ *Per serving: 237 calories, 22 g protein, 14 g carbohydrates, 11 g total fat (3 g saturated fat), 54 mg cholesterol, 208 mg sodium*

Smoked Pork Chops with Prune Plums

Preparation time: About 10 minutes

Cooking time: 16 to 18 minutes

Juicy purple plums cooked in lemon juice and honey dress up these quick-cooking smoked chops. A touch of dried red chiles adds zest. Offer with fluffy rice to soak up the ample sauce.

- 4 **smoked pork loin chops (about 1¼ pounds *total*), trimmed of fat**
- 1½ **teaspoons grated lemon peel**
- 3 **tablespoons lemon juice**
- 2 **tablespoons honey**
- ⅛ **teaspoon crushed dried hot red chiles (optional)**
- ⅔ **cup regular-strength beef broth**
- 2 **teaspoons cornstarch**
- 12 **prune plums (about 12 oz. *total*), halved and pitted**

Heat a wide nonstick frying pan over medium-high heat. Add pork chops and brown on both sides, turning once (8 to 10 minutes *total*). Meanwhile, in a small bowl, combine lemon peel, lemon juice, honey, chiles (if used), and all but 2 tablespoons of the beef broth. Pour lemon mixture over chops in pan. Cover, reduce heat, and simmer for 5 minutes. Meanwhile, blend reserved 2 tablespoons of broth and cornstarch; set aside.

Add plums to pork chops, cover, and simmer until plums are hot (about 3 minutes). Using a slotted spoon, lift chops and plums onto a platter and keep warm. Blend cornstarch mixture into cooking liquid. Increase heat to high and cook, stirring constantly, until sauce has thickened and is bubbling. Spoon over chops and plums. Makes 4 servings.

■ *Per serving: 253 calories, 23 g protein, 28 g carbohydrates, 6 g total fat (2 g saturated fat), 53 mg cholesterol, 1,764 mg sodium*

Slow-cooked Pork & Beans

Preparation time: About 10 minutes

Standing time: 1 hour

Cooking time: 2 to 2½ hours (on range top) or 8 to 12 hours (in slow cooker)

Cook this hearty soup-stew in a slow cooker or on top of the range in a capacious kettle. Ladle it into wide, shallow bowls, and serve with your favorite spinach salad and a loaf of crusty bread.

- 1 **pound Great Northern beans or small white beans, sorted, rinsed, and drained**
- 1 **can (8 oz.) pineapple chunks**
- 2½ **cups water**
- 1 **clove garlic, minced or pressed**
- ⅓ **cup soy sauce**
- ¼ **cup lemon juice**
- 3 **tablespoons molasses or honey**
- 2 **teaspoons chili powder**
- 1 **teaspoon *each* ground cumin and ground ginger**
- ¼ **teaspoon pepper**
- 8 **thin pork rib chops (about 2½ lbs. *total*), trimmed of fat**

In a 5-quart pan, bring 2 quarts water to a boil over high heat. Add beans and boil for 2 minutes. Remove from heat, cover, and let stand for 1 hour; then drain and rinse.

Drain pineapple, reserving juice; set fruit aside. In a wide 6-quart pan or a 6-quart electric slow cooker, mix beans, juice from pineapple, water, garlic, soy sauce, lemon juice, molasses, chili powder, cumin, ginger, and pepper. Nestle pork chops in bean mixture.

If using a 6-quart pan, bring to a boil over medium-high heat, cover, reduce heat to medium-low, and simmer until pork and beans are very tender when pierced (2 to 2½ hours); if using a slow cooker, cover and cook at low setting until pork and beans are very tender when pierced (8 to 12 hours).

Skim and discard surface fat, if necessary. Stir in pineapple chunks (don't worry about breaking up pork chops; this distributes meat more evenly). Cook just until heated through (about 5 minutes). Makes 8 servings.

■ *Per serving: 401 calories, 35 g protein, 47 g carbohydrates, 8 g total fat (3 g saturated fat), 55 mg cholesterol, 741 mg sodium*

Bistro-style Pork Chops & Lentils

Preparation time: About 15 minutes

Cooking time: About 6 minutes

Baking time: About 1½ hours

This substantial casserole pairs savory lentils and juicy rib chops. To complete the menu, warm a crusty whole-wheat baguette in the oven during the last few minutes of baking time and steam coarsely chopped Swiss chard or whole leaf spinach.

- 1 **cup lentils, rinsed and drained**
- 1 **clove garlic, minced or pressed**
- 1 **small onion, thinly sliced**
- 1 **medium-size carrot (about 3 oz.), shredded**
- ¼ **teaspoon *each* salt and dry rosemary**
- ⅛ **teaspoon white pepper**
- ¼ **cup chopped parsley**
- 1 **can (14½ oz.) regular-strength beef broth**
- 1 **cup dry white wine**
- 1 **tablespoon *each* tomato paste and Dijon mustard**
- 4 **pork rib chops (about 1¼ lbs. *total*), trimmed of fat**

In a 3-quart casserole, mix lentils, garlic, onion, carrot, salt, rosemary, pepper, and all but 1 tablespoon of the parsley. In a small pan, combine beef broth, wine, tomato paste, and mustard. Place pan over medium heat and stir until mustard has dissolved and mixture is boiling; pour over lentil mixture. Cover and bake in a 350° oven until lentils are almost tender (about 1¼ hours).

Shortly before lentils are tender, heat a wide nonstick frying pan over medium-high heat. Add pork chops and brown well on both sides, turning once (about 6 minutes *total*). Place chops atop lentils in casserole, cover, and return to oven. Continue baking until lentils are very tender (about 15 more minutes). Garnish with remaining 1 tablespoon parsley. Makes 4 servings.

■ *Per serving: 358 calories, 37 g protein, 33 g carbohydrates, 9 g total fat (3 g saturated fat), 55 mg cholesterol, 717 mg sodium*

*Swathed in a robust tomato sauce, Roman Oven-braised
Bones (recipe on page 88) are lean and luscious. Cooked entirely in
the oven, from the browning to the moist simmering with dried
mushrooms, this southern version of osso buco teams nicely
with long fusilli pasta and a green salad.*

Veal

Round
Loin
Rib
Shoulder
Ground Veal

Veal has long been prized for its delicate flavor and tenderness. Its low calorie and fat content makes it a popular choice for the discriminating and health-conscious cook.

Because it has so little surface fat—and virtually no marbling—it must be cooked carefully to retain its juiciness and to avoid toughening.

See the illustration on page 84 for more information about the leanest cuts of veal.

Lean Veal Cuts

Round. Veal round or leg accounts for most of the meat that's sold for scaloppine and cutlets. It can be pounded for added tenderness, if desired, and cooked quickly by either dry heat (sautéing or panfrying with a minimum of fat) or moist heat (braising in your choice of liquid). It's sometimes boned, rolled, and sold as a leg roast (slow cooking in a liquid will preserve its succulence).

Loin. Bone-in cuts from the veal loin look like miniatures of corresponding beef cuts—but they're usually called chops, rather than steaks. Boneless cuts may be called by such cosmopolitan-sounding names as noisettes, scallops, or medallions. This very tender cut can be cooked by dry-heat methods such as sautéing or grilling. Loin roasts are best prepared by roasting, uncovered, with no added liquid.

Rib. Most veal rib comes to market as chops, either boneless or bone-in. This is also the section from which a veal crown roast can be created. These small chops can be quickly sautéed, broiled, grilled, or cooked gently in a savory liquid.

Shoulder. Unlike beef shoulder cuts, most of which are too high in fat to get under the lowfat wire, veal shoulder is a good source of lean meat. Much is sold already boned and cubed for stew. If you don't mind taking time to cut the meat at home, it's often more economical to buy a boneless shoulder roast for such dishes. Slowly cooked using moist heat, on top of the range or in the oven, a rolled, boneless shoulder roast makes a fork-tender entrée that serves six to eight people generously.

Ground Veal. Ground veal can come from virtually any cut—though it's frequently meat from the flank. Cook it as you would any other ground meat or poultry. Because it's very low in fat, avoid cooking it at an overly hot temperature; you may need to add some moisture.

Veal Scallops with Red Onion Marmalade

Preparation time: About 20 minutes

Cooking time: About 25 minutes

Slather tart-sweet red onion relish over these easy veal scallops. Serve with sautéed summer squash.

    Red Onion Marmalade (recipe follows)
 1 to 1¼ pounds boneless veal round steak
    (about ½ inch thick), trimmed of fat
    White pepper
    Freshly ground nutmeg
 1½ to 2 tablespoons all-purpose flour
 1 tablespoon margarine
 1 teaspoon Dijon mustard
 ¼ cup dry white wine
    Salt

Prepare Red Onion Marmalade. Cut veal into 4 servings. Place between sheets of plastic wrap and pound with flat side of a meat mallet until ¼ inch thick. Remove plastic wrap and sprinkle veal with pepper and nutmeg; dust with flour, tapping to remove excess.

Melt margarine in a wide nonstick frying pan over medium-high heat until it bubbles. Add veal; cook, turning once, until browned on both sides (3 to 5 minutes *total*); then transfer to a platter and keep warm.

Add mustard and wine to pan drippings, stirring until mixture is boiling rapidly; pour over veal. Season to taste with salt. Spoon on half of the marmalade. Serve with remaining marmalade. Makes 4 servings.

■ *Per serving: 235 calories, 28 g protein, 11 g carbohydrates, 7 g total fat (1 g saturated fat), 100 mg cholesterol, 172 mg sodium*

Red Onion Marmalade. Melt 1 tablespoon **margarine** in a wide nonstick frying pan over medium-high heat. Mix in 1 pound **red onions** (thinly sliced), 2½ tablespoons **sugar**, and ¼ teaspoon **white pepper.** Cover and cook, stirring occasionally, until onions are very soft and juices have evaporated (6 to 8 minutes). Stir in ½ cup **dry white wine** and ¼ cup **red wine vinegar;** reduce heat to medium and cook, uncovered, stirring occasionally, until liquid has evaporated (10 to 12 minutes). If made ahead, you may let cool, cover, and refrigerate for up to 3 days; reheat to serve. Makes about 1¼ cups.

■ *Per tablespoon: 20 calories, 0 g protein, 3 g carbohydrates, 1 g total fat (0 g saturated fat), 0 mg cholesterol, 7 mg sodium*

Eggplant-stuffed Veal Rolls

Preparation time: About 30 minutes

Cooking time: About 45 minutes

Eggplant, spinach, bread crumbs, sage, and a touch of cheese make a savory stuffing for petite veal rolls.

 1 small eggplant (about 12 oz.), unpeeled
    Olive oil cooking spray
 1½ tablespoons olive oil
 1 small onion, finely chopped
 ¼ teaspoon dry sage leaves
 1 clove garlic, minced or pressed
 2 cups coarsely chopped spinach leaves
 ½ cup soft bread crumbs
 ¼ teaspoon *each* salt and ground nutmeg
 ½ cup grated Parmesan cheese
 ¾ cup plus 2 tablespoons dry white wine
 1½ pounds boneless veal round steak (about
    ¼ inch thick), trimmed of fat
 1½ to 2 tablespoons all-purpose flour
 6 ounces mushrooms, thinly sliced

Cut eggplant into ½-inch cubes. Spread in a greased shallow, rimmed baking pan; coat with cooking spray.

Bake in a 425° oven until well browned (20 to 25 minutes). Meanwhile, heat 1 tablespoon of the olive oil in a wide frying pan over medium heat; add onion and sage. Cook until onion is soft (about 5 minutes). Stir in garlic and spinach; continue cooking until spinach has wilted (about 1 minute). Remove from heat and mix in eggplant, bread crumbs, salt, nutmeg, cheese, and 2 tablespoons of the wine. Set aside.

Cut veal into 12 portions. Place between sheets of plastic wrap; pound with flat side of a meat mallet until almost doubled in size. Place about 2 heaping tablespoons of eggplant mixture on each, tuck in sides, and roll up compactly; fasten with skewers. Dust veal rolls with flour.

Heat remaining ½ tablespoon olive oil in a wide nonstick frying pan over medium-high heat. Add veal; brown well. Add mushrooms and remaining wine. Cover, reduce heat to low, and simmer until veal is very tender (about 20 minutes). Lift out veal, arrange on a platter, and keep warm. Increase heat to high, bring mushroom mixture to a boil, and cook, uncovered, stirring, until slightly thickened (2 to 3 minutes). Spoon sauce over veal. Makes 6 servings.

■ *Per serving: 232 calories, 29 g protein, 10 g carbohydrates, 8 g total fat (2 g saturated fat), 94 mg cholesterol, 325 mg sodium*

Herb-stuffed Veal Leg in Piperade

Preparation time: About 35 minutes

Cooking time: 30 to 35 minutes

Baking time: 1¼ to 1½ hours

Piperade, a vibrant Basque sauce of tomatoes and bell peppers, tops this parsley- and basil-stuffed roast.

   Parsley & Basil Filling (recipe follows)
1 boneless veal leg roast (2 to 2½ pounds)
2 teaspoons olive oil
1 small onion, finely chopped
¼ cup (about 2 oz.) finely chopped smoked pork loin, trimmed of fat
1 *each* small green and red bell pepper (about 4 oz. *each*), seeded and cut into thin strips
1 can (about 1 lb.) tomatoes
¼ teaspoon salt
⅛ teaspoon pepper

Prepare Parsley & Basil Filling. Open out veal; butterfly, if necessary, to achieve a rectangular shape. Spread filling over surface of veal. Roll compactly, starting with a short edge. Tie with string at 1½-inch intervals.

Heat 1 teaspoon of the oil in a wide nonstick frying pan over medium-high heat. Add veal roast and brown on all sides, turning as needed. Lift roast out and transfer to a shallow 3- to 4-quart casserole; set aside.

Add remaining 1 teaspoon oil to same pan; reduce heat to medium. Stir in onion, pork, and bell peppers; cook, stirring often, until vegetables are soft but not brown (5 to 7 minutes). Add tomatoes (break up with a spoon) and their liquid, salt, and pepper; bring to a boil. Cover, reduce heat, and simmer for 15 minutes. Pour mixture over veal. Cover and bake in a 350° oven until veal is very tender (1¼ to 1½ hours).

Lift veal onto a deep platter; cover lightly to keep warm. Transfer tomato mixture to a 2-quart pan; then bring to a boil over medium-high heat. Cook, stirring, until slightly thickened (5 to 8 minutes). Cut veal into ½-inch-thick slices and top with some of the tomato sauce. Serve with remaining sauce. Makes 8 servings.

Parsley & Basil Filling. Mix 1 teaspoon *each* **olive oil** and **lemon juice;** ½ cup finely chopped **parsley;** 2 cloves **garlic** (minced or pressed); ¼ cup *each* coarsely chopped **fresh basil leaves** and **soft bread crumbs;** and ½ teaspoon grated **lemon peel.**

- *Per serving: 187 calories, 30 g protein, 6 g carbohydrates, 5 g total fat (1 g saturated fat), 103 mg cholesterol, 348 mg sodium*

- *Pictured on facing page*

Grilled Veal Chops with Ratatouille

Preparation time: About 35 minutes

Cooking time: About 10 minutes

Baking time: About 2 hours

Quick-cooking veal chops share center stage with an oven-baked ratatouille seasoned with fresh basil.

   Oven Ratatouille (recipe follows)
2 teaspoons lemon juice
1 teaspoon olive oil
1 tablespoon chopped fresh thyme leaves or ½ teaspoon dry thyme leaves
1 clove garlic, minced or pressed
4 veal loin chops, about ¾ inch thick (about 1¼ lbs. *total*), trimmed of fat
   Olive oil cooking spray
   Salt and freshly ground pepper
   Lemon zest
   Thyme sprigs (optional)

Prepare Oven Ratatouille. When it's nearly done, mix lemon juice, oil, thyme, and garlic. Drizzle mixture over veal chops on both sides, rubbing in with a spoon.

Spray a ridged cooktop grill pan with cooking spray. Place over medium-high heat and preheat until a drop of water dances on surface. Place chops on grill pan and cook, turning once, until well browned and barely pink inside when cut near bone (6 to 8 minutes *total*). Season to taste with salt and pepper. Garnish chops with lemon zest and, if desired, thyme sprigs. Serve with ratatouille. Makes 4 servings.

Oven Ratatouille. Cut a small (about 12 oz.) unpeeled **eggplant** into ½- by 2-inch sticks; cut 1 *each* large **yellow and green zucchini** (or 2 green zucchini; about 12 oz. *total*) into ½-inch slices. Quarter 1 pound **Roma-style tomatoes** lengthwise. In a deep 3- to 4-quart casserole, mix cut vegetables with 1 medium-size **onion** (finely chopped), ⅔ cup chopped **fresh basil leaves,** 2 cloves **garlic** (minced or pressed), and 2 teaspoons **olive oil.** Cover and bake in a 400° oven for 1¾ hours. Uncover, stir gently, and continue baking until eggplant is creamy and most of the juices have evaporated (about 15 minutes). Season to taste with **salt** and **pepper.**

- *Per serving: 219 calories, 21 g protein, 17 g carbohydrates, 9 g total fat (2 g saturated fat), 69 mg cholesterol, 80 mg sodium*

*Lemon, garlic, and fresh thyme enliven simple Grilled
Veal Chops with Ratatouille (recipe on facing page), a colorful Provençal
vegetable casserole. Stuff mushroom caps with spinach, bread crumbs,
and a little Parmesan cheese to bake as an accompaniment.*

Feature

Italian Braised Veal

Savory veal dishes are a staple in Italian cuisine, and many of them fit neatly within the limits of lowfat cooking. Others that conventionally contain generous amounts of butter and oil can be modified to reduce the quantity required.

Oven-braising works its moist-heat magic on such less-tender cuts as veal shanks and breast. You can also braise a veal shoulder roast in a big, deep pan on the rangetop for a lean but impressive reward.

■ *Pictured on page 82*

Roman Oven-braised Bones

½ ounce dried European mushrooms
1 cup hot water
6 veal shanks (5½ to 6 lbs. *total*), cut crosswise into 3-inch sections
1 can (8 oz.) tomato sauce
1 can (6 oz.) tomato paste
1 can (14½ oz.) regular-strength chicken broth
1 large onion, finely chopped
2 cloves garlic, minced or pressed
1 large carrot (about 4 oz.), finely chopped
¾ teaspoon ground cinnamon
1 teaspoon dry basil
  Salt
  Italian parsley sprigs
¼ to ⅓ cup freshly grated Parmesan cheese

Place mushrooms in a small bowl and cover with hot water; let stand until soft (about 30 minutes).

Meanwhile, place veal shanks in a single layer in a 5-quart (about 11 by 15 inches) pan or baking dish. Bake, uncovered, in a 400° oven until browned (about

35 minutes). In a large bowl, combine tomato sauce, tomato paste, and chicken broth; set aside.

Remove pan from oven and turn shanks over. Drain mushrooms, reserving all but last bit of water with residue. Sprinkle veal with mushrooms, onion, garlic, carrot, cinnamon, and basil. Add reserved mushroom liquid to tomato sauce mixture and pour over veal. Cover tightly with foil, return to oven, and bake until veal is very tender when pierced with a fork and pulls easily from bones (1½ to 2 hours).

Lift veal onto a serving dish; cover lightly to keep warm. Skim and discard fat from cooking liquid, if necessary. If liquid exceeds 2½ cups, pour into a wide frying pan and bring to a boil over medium-high heat; cook, stirring often, until reduced to about 2½ cups. Season to taste with salt; then pour sauce over veal. Garnish with parsley and serve with Parmesan cheese. Makes 6 servings.

■ *Per serving: 399 calories, 66 g protein, 15 g carbohydrates, 7 g total fat (2 g saturated fat), 228 mg cholesterol, 1,031 mg sodium*

■ *Pictured on page 95*

Pasta & Red Pepper–stuffed Veal Breast

  Orzo & Red Pepper Stuffing (recipe follows)
2¾ to 3 pounds veal breast
  Olive oil cooking spray
  Coarsely ground pepper
¼ teaspoon dry thyme leaves
3 chicken bouillon cubes dissolved in 3 cups hot water
½ cup dry sherry
  Sage sprigs (optional)

Prepare Orzo & Red Pepper Stuffing.

Cut a pocket in veal breast for stuffing. To cut the pocket, lay breast, bone side down, on flat surface. Pull the breast apart at the membrane, separating it at natural opening. Then use a knife to slit veal almost through to other side. (Or, at time of purchase, ask your butcher to cut pocket for you.)

Fill pocket with stuffing. Pull edge of pocket over stuffing; fasten open edge with metal skewers or sew closed with a heavy needle and string, taking a stitch between each rib.

Coat a large shallow roasting pan with cooking spray. Place veal breast, bone side up, in pan. Spray with cooking spray; then sprinkle with pepper and thyme. Pour bouillon mixture and sherry around veal. Cover tightly with foil and bake in a 375° oven until very tender when pierced (about 2 hours). Uncover; continue baking until top is richly browned (about 20 minutes).

Lift veal onto a board or platter, cover lightly to keep warm, and let stand for about 10 minutes. If more than ½ cup liquid remains in roasting pan, place pan over medium-high heat and bring to a boil, stirring constantly, until reduced to about ½ cup.

Cut veal breast between ribs; serve with pan liquid. Garnish with sage sprigs, if desired. Makes 8 servings.

Orzo & Red Pepper Stuffing. Heat 1 tablespoon **olive oil** in a 3-quart pan over medium heat. Add 1 small **onion** (finely chopped); cook, stirring often, until soft but not brown (3 to 5 minutes). Stir in ¼ pound **mushrooms** (thinly sliced), 1 medium-size (about 6 oz.) **red bell pepper** (seeded and finely chopped), and 1 clove **garlic** (minced or pressed); cook, stirring often, until mushrooms are soft (8 to 10 minutes).

Stir in 1 cup (about 8 oz.) **dry rice-shaped pasta.** Add 1 can (14½ oz.) **regular-strength chicken broth.** Bring to a boil; then boil gently, uncovered, stirring often, until broth is absorbed but pasta is still slightly chewy (about 10 minutes). Remove from heat and stir in 2 cups coarsely chopped **fresh spinach leaves,** ¼ cup chopped **fresh sage leaves** (or 1 tablespoon dry sage leaves), and ¼ cup grated **Parmesan cheese.** Season to taste with **salt** and **pepper.** Cover; let stand for 10 minutes.

■ *Per serving: 321 calories, 26 g protein, 28 g carbohydrates, 11 g total fat (4 g saturated fat), 86 mg cholesterol, 794 mg sodium*

Veal Shoulder with Sun-dried Tomatoes

    ½ cup dried tomatoes
    2 cups warm water
    1 boneless veal shoulder roast (1¾ to 2 lbs.), trimmed of fat
    12 fresh sage leaves or 1 teaspoon dried sage leaves
    1 tablespoon olive oil
    1 medium-size onion, thinly sliced
    1 cup dry white wine
    ½ cup chopped parsley
    1½ tablespoons grated lemon peel
    2 cloves garlic, minced or pressed
      Salt and white pepper

In a medium-size bowl, soak tomatoes in warm water to cover until soft (about 1 hour). Drain well, reserving 1 cup of the soaking liquid. Cut tomatoes into ½-inch-wide strips; set aside.

Open out veal; butterfly if necessary, to achieve a rectangular shape. Place between sheets of plastic wrap and pound with flat side of a meat mallet until about ½ inch thick. Remove plastic wrap; cover veal with sage leaves and tomato strips, leaving about a 1-inch margin on all sides. Roll compactly, starting with a short edge. Tie with string at 1½-inch intervals.

Heat oil in a deep, wide nonstick pan over medium-high heat. Add veal roast and brown on all sides, turning as needed. When you turn to brown last side, add onion slices to pan. When onions are soft and lightly browned (about 3 minutes), stir in wine and reserved tomato-soaking liquid. Bring to a boil, cover, and reduce heat to low. Simmer, carefully turning veal in cooking liquid once or twice, until veal is very tender when pierced (1½ to 2 hours).

Meanwhile, in a small bowl, combine parsley, lemon peel, and garlic; set aside.

Lift veal onto a deep platter and cover lightly to keep warm. To cooking liquid, add half of the parsley mixture; bring to a boil over medium-high heat. Cook, stirring often, until reduced by about a third; season to taste with salt and pepper. Cut veal into about ½-inch-thick slices. Spoon some of the parsley sauce over veal; serve with remaining sauce and parsley mixture to add to taste. Makes 6 servings.

■ *Per serving: 207 calories, 29 g protein, 6 g carbohydrates, 7 g total fat (2 g saturated fat), 122 mg cholesterol, 143 mg sodium*

*Neoclassical Blanquette de Veau (recipe on facing page) departs
widely from the French original. Puréed vegetables substitute for cream and
egg yolks to enrich the sauce that clings to tender veal morsels. Steamed
baby carrots and brussels sprouts go well with this entrée.*

Rib Chops Niçoise

Preparation time: About 10 minutes

Cooking time: About 1 hour

Diminutive veal rib chops simmer to moist tenderness in a savory tomato, basil, and olive sauce—a bit of the south of France brought home.

- 1 tablespoon olive oil
- 8 small veal rib chops (about 1⅓ lbs. *total*), trimmed of fat
- ¼ cup thinly sliced shallots
- 2 cloves garlic, minced or pressed
- 1 can (14½ oz.) pear-shaped tomatoes
- ½ cup white Zinfandel or dry rosé wine
- ½ cup slivered fresh basil leaves or 1½ tablespoons dry basil leaves
- ¼ cup Niçoise olives or small ripe olives
  Salt

Heat oil in a wide nonstick frying pan over medium-high heat. Add veal chops and brown well on both sides, turning once (about 6 minutes *total*); remove from pan and set aside.

To pan, add shallots and cook, stirring often, until soft and beginning to brown (about 2 minutes). Stir in garlic, tomatoes (break up with a spoon) and their liquid, wine, and basil; bring to a boil. Return chops to pan and sprinkle with olives. Reduce heat to low, cover, and simmer until veal is very tender when pierced (35 to 40 minutes).

Increase heat to medium and boil gently, uncovered, stirring occasionally, until liquid is slightly reduced (8 to 10 minutes). Season to taste with salt. Makes 4 servings.

■ *Per serving: 184 calories, 20 g protein, 8 g carbohydrates, 8 g total fat (2 g saturated fat), 75 mg cholesterol, 331 mg sodium*

■ *Pictured on facing page*

Neoclassical Blanquette de Veau

Preparation time: About 30 minutes

Cooking time: About 1½ hours

In classic French cuisine, *blanquette de veau* relies on butter, cream, and egg yolks. This version substitutes a flavorful purée of vegetables.

- 2 pounds boneless veal shoulder, trimmed of fat
- 1 tablespoon margarine
- 2 medium-size onions, finely chopped
- ¼ cup chopped shallots
- 1 medium-size carrot, finely chopped
- 2 sprigs *each* parsley and tarragon, tied together with string
- 2 leeks (white parts only), thinly sliced
- 3 tablespoons lemon juice
- ½ teaspoon salt
- ⅛ teaspoon ground white pepper
- 1 medium-size (about 8 oz.) thin-skinned potato, peeled and quartered
- ½ cup *each* dry white wine and regular-strength chicken broth
- ½ cup evaporated skim milk
- ⅛ teaspoon ground nutmeg
- 1 package (9 oz.) frozen artichoke hearts
- ½ cup thawed frozen peas
  Tarragon sprigs (optional)

Cut veal into 1¼-inch cubes; set aside. Melt margarine in a wide 3½- to 4-quart pan over medium heat. Add onions, shallots, and carrot; cook, stirring often, until onions are soft but not brown (about 5 minutes). Stir in parsley-tarragon bundle, leeks, veal, lemon juice, salt, pepper, potato, wine, and chicken broth; bring to a boil. Cover, reduce heat to low, and simmer until veal is very tender when pierced (1 to 1½ hours).

Using a slotted spoon, lift veal and most of the vegetables from cooking liquid and transfer to a bowl. Remove and discard parsley-tarragon bundle. Bring cooking liquid to a boil over high heat. Boil, stirring occasionally, until reduced to about 1¼ cups.

Meanwhile, separate vegetables from veal. Place vegetables in a food processor or blender with about ¼ cup of the cooking liquid; whirl until puréed. Add purée to reduced cooking liquid; blend in milk and nutmeg. Bring to a gentle boil over medium heat, stirring often. Blend in veal; then reduce heat to low, cover, and keep warm.

Cook artichokes according to package directions; drain and cut into bite-size pieces. Add artichokes and peas to veal mixture. Cook, stirring, over low heat just until heated through (2 to 3 minutes). Season to taste with salt and garnish with tarragon, if desired. Makes 6 to 8 servings.

■ *Per serving: 251 calories, 30 g protein, 18 g carbohydrates, 6 g total fat (1 g saturated fat), 112 mg cholesterol, 427 mg sodium*

Braised Veal with Escarole

Preparation time: About 20 minutes

Cooking time: About 1¾ hours

While escarole is usually found raw in salads, here it's cooked in a hot veal stew of Italian origin. Present with a pasta that will capture the tart sauce, such as corkscrew-shaped *rotelle* or *orecchiette* (little ears).

    2 pounds boneless veal shoulder, trimmed
       of fat
    1 large onion, finely chopped
    1 tablespoon olive oil
    1 cup water
    1 large carrot (about 4 oz.), finely chopped
    1 cup dry white wine
    ½ teaspoon salt
    ⅛ teaspoon *each* ground nutmeg and white
       pepper
    2 quarts lightly packed shredded escarole
    2 teaspoons cornstarch blended with ¼ cup
       water
       Lemon wedges

Cut veal into 1-inch cubes. In a wide 3½- to 4-quart pan, combine veal, onion, oil, and ½ cup of the water over medium-low heat. Cover and simmer for 30 minutes. Increase heat to medium and cook, uncovered, stirring occasionally, until onions are brown and most of the liquid has evaporated (about 30 minutes). Add remaining ½ cup water, carrot, wine, salt, nutmeg, and pepper, stirring to loosen any browned bits from pan. Cover, reduce heat to low, and simmer until veal is tender when pierced (35 to 45 more minutes).

Increase heat to medium and add escarole, about half at a time, stirring until it wilts (about 3 minutes). Blend in cornstarch mixture and cook, uncovered, stirring constantly, until stew is boiling and has thickened (about 3 minutes). Season to taste with lemon. Makes 6 to 8 servings.

■ *Per serving: 191 calories, 27 g protein, 6 g carbohydrates, 6 g total fat (1 g saturated fat), 112 mg cholesterol, 296 mg sodium*

Veal Stew with Caraway

Preparation time: About 15 minutes

Cooking time: About 1¾ hours

This tender, delicate veal stew is at its best when served atop a mound of golden egg noodles.

    1 to 1½ pounds boneless veal shoulder
    1 tablespoon salad oil
    ¼ teaspoon salt
    ⅛ teaspoon white pepper
    1 large onion, finely chopped
    ½ cup dry white wine
    2 teaspoons caraway seeds
    1 can (14½ oz.) regular-strength chicken
       broth
    2 medium-size carrots (about 6 oz. *total*),
       chopped
       Chopped parsley

Cut veal into 1-inch cubes. In a wide 3½- to 4-quart pan, combine veal, oil, salt, pepper, onion, and wine over medium-low heat. Cover and simmer for 30 minutes. Stir in caraway seeds, increase heat to medium, and cook, uncovered, stirring occasionally, until onions are brown and most of the liquid has evaporated (15 to 20 minutes). Add chicken broth and carrots, stirring to loosen any browned bits from pan.

Cover, reduce heat to low, and simmer until veal is tender when pierced (35 to 45 more minutes). Increase heat to medium and cook, uncovered, until thickened slightly (12 to 15 minutes). Garnish with parsley. Makes 4 to 6 servings.

■ *Per serving: 191 calories, 24 g protein, 7 g carbohydrates, 7 g total fat (1 g saturated fat), 98 mg cholesterol, 584 mg sodium*

Linguine with Veal Peperonata

Preparation time: About 25 minutes

Baking time: About 15 minutes

Cooking time: About 10 minutes

Diminutive meatballs dot a tricolored tangle of bell peppers flavored with lemon juice, garlic, and capers.

- 1 egg white
- ⅓ cup evaporated skim milk
- 2 tablespoons all-purpose flour
- 1 small onion, finely chopped
- ⅛ teaspoon ground nutmeg
- ⅓ cup finely chopped parsley
- 1 pound ground veal
- 1 tablespoon olive oil
- 1 *each* medium-size red, green, and yellow bell pepper (about 6 oz. *each*), seeded and cut into thin strips
- ½ teaspoon Italian herb seasoning or ⅛ teaspoon *each* dry basil, oregano, thyme, and marjoram
- 1 package (9 oz.) fresh linguine
- 1 clove garlic, minced or pressed
- 2 tablespoons lemon juice
- 2 teaspoons drained capers plus 1 tablespoon of the liquid
- 1 tablespoon red wine vinegar

In a medium-size bowl, beat together egg white and evaporated milk. Blend in flour, onion, nutmeg, and ¼ cup of the parsley; then lightly mix in veal. Shape mixture into 1-inch balls. Place slightly apart in a greased shallow baking pan. Bake, uncovered, in a 450° oven until well browned (about 15 minutes).

While meatballs are baking, heat oil in a wide non-stick frying pan over medium heat. Add bell peppers and Italian herbs; stir until peppers are just softened but not browned (about 5 minutes).

Meanwhile, in a 5- to 6-quart pan, cook linguine in 3 quarts boiling water just until tender (1 to 2 minutes); or cook according to package directions.

To pepper mixture, add meatballs and garlic; stir carefully until meatballs are heated through (2 to 3 minutes). Gently mix in lemon juice, capers, caper liquid, and vinegar.

Drain linguine and top with meatballs and peppers. Garnish with remaining parsley. Makes 4 servings.

■ *Per serving: 432 calories, 33 g protein, 48 g carbohydrates, 12 g total fat (3 g saturated fat), 154 mg cholesterol, 172 mg sodium*

Veal & Mushroom Patties

Preparation time: About 25 minutes

Cooking time: About 30 minutes

Very finely chopped mushrooms and tomato lend savory substance to these delicate veal patties.

- 1½ tablespoons margarine
- 1 small onion, finely chopped
- 6 ounces mushrooms, very finely chopped
- ½ teaspoon dry thyme leaves
- ¼ cup chopped parsley
- 1 clove garlic, minced or pressed
- 1 small firm-ripe tomato, peeled, seeded, and finely chopped
- ¼ teaspoon pepper
- 1 egg white
- ¾ cup regular-strength beef broth
- ⅓ cup fine dry bread crumbs
- 1 pound ground veal

Melt ½ tablespoon of the margarine in a wide non-stick frying pan over medium-high heat. Add onion, mushrooms, thyme, and parsley; cook, stirring often, until mushrooms begin to brown and liquid has evaporated (about 5 minutes). Stir in garlic, tomato, and pepper; continue stirring until mixture is almost dry. Remove from heat and let cool for 5 minutes.

Meanwhile, in a medium-size bowl, beat egg white with ¼ cup of the beef broth; stir in bread crumbs and veal. Add mushroom mixture and mix lightly until well combined. Shape mixture into 6 patties, each about ¾ inch thick.

In same frying pan, melt remaining 1 tablespoon margarine over medium heat. Add veal patties and cook, turning once, until well browned on outside and no longer pink in center when cut (15 to 18 minutes *total*). Lift patties onto a platter and keep warm. To pan, add remaining ½ cup broth. Increase heat to high, stirring to loosen any browned bits from pan; boil until reduced by about half. Pour over veal patties. Makes 6 servings.

■ *Per serving: 176 calories, 17 g protein, 7 g carbohydrates, 9 g total fat (3 g saturated fat), 62 mg cholesterol, 252 mg sodium*

INDEX

This hearty Italian dish, Pasta & Red Pepper-stuffed Veal
Breast (recipe on page 88), is oven-braised in sherry and chicken
broth. Fill the pocket in the veal with rice-shaped pasta (or orzo)
cooked in broth with mushrooms, garlic, and onion.